Weapons of Our Warfare

By Dr. Ernest Maddox

Weapons of Our Warfare

© **Copyright 2013 Dr. Ernest Maddox**
Frist Edition
Unauthorized duplication prohibited

P.O. Box 48547, Oak Park, MI. 48237
Phone: 248.796.8523
Email: dr.ernest.maddox@gmail.com
Website: dremaddox.org

Scripture quotations are "NKJV" (unless marked otherwise) are taken from the New King James Version. Copyright 1982 by Thomas Nelson, Inc.

Scripture quotations marked "KJV" are in the public domain.

ISBN 978-0-9779748-5-6

Weapons of Our Warfare

Welcome

You have purchased this book and you are in for a very unique experience. This book or should I say narrative is a result of over three hours of lecture regarding spiritual warfare. I decided that this book/narrative should reflect the cadence and the speaking approach that I used in creating the three CDs entitled, "Weapons of Our Warfare." What is unique about this is that you can read the book, listen to the CDs, or do them together.

This book is laid out in such a way that you will be able to identify what I call track categories. At the beginning of each new thought, there is a timing signature indicating where this particular subject matter is located on the audio CD. You will notice that there may be some time signatures identifying a particular subject congregated under a track number. Track numbers are represented as T-1, T-2, etc., for the purpose of coordination.

To simplify the process, the book is broken down into three major sections, to correspond with the three CDs, (Weapons of Our Warfare disks 1, 2, and 3). Each lecture section will have its own track and time code layout. This book and the CDs are purchased separately, unless specified otherwise during the purchasing process. Both items contain the exact same information, it is just a matter of preference.

Weapons of Our Warfare

Weapons of Our Warfare Section One

Weapons of Our Warfare Section One

Weapons of Our Warfare Section One

Table of Contents

Lecture Section One..1
    Introduction T-1...5
    Foundational Aspects T-2 5
    Second Point of Attack –Adam and Eve T-3.................8
    Next Attack-The Children T-4.......................................12
    Old Testament Demonic Impact or Influence T-5...13
        An Episode with David 13
    An Episode with Job T-6 14
        Leviathan 15
    New Testament Demonic Impact
    or Influence T-7..16
        Caution..17
        Luke 4:18-19 18
        Luke 4:31 18
        Impacts Men and Women 19
    Multiple Possession T-8 19
        Impacts Children, Also 20
    Apostle Paul T-9 20
        Ephesians 6:10-14.....................................20
        II Corinthians 10:3-5 21
        II Corinthians 11:13-15 22
        Timothy 4:1-2 22
        Acts 8:1-7 23
    Conclusion T-10 24

    Section Two……………………….…..............................28

    Section Three…………………………….…..................57

    References and Recommended Readings…….……..89

    Appendix A Impact of a Deliverance Prayer…..........91

    Short Biography…....……………………….............106

Weapons of Our Warfare Section One

Introduction (T- 1)

Hello, my name is Dr. Ernest Maddox. I'm the pastor of the POINTE of Light Christian Center. We are located in Detroit, Michigan. And you know if you have purchased this CD, or it's been made a gift to you by a friend, you are in for a blessing.

Our topic is going to be in the area of spiritual warfare. If you are interested in a title, you can call it the ***Weapons of Our Warfare***.

But we are going to be talking about spiritual and supernatural activity relative to the Word of God, and how it impacts the Christian. And we are going to approach it from a foundational point of attack, an influence issue relative to those of us who are walking in the context of Christianity relative to God, the Father, the Son and the Holy Spirit.

And without further ado I will encourage you right now at this moment to go ahead and get your Bibles, something to write with and a notebook. Because you will want to be able to write down some of this information even though you may own the CD. You may want to document some of the references for later study. So why don't we just go right into the foundational aspects of what we are talking about here.

Foundational Aspects (1:44 T-2)

Let's go to Revelation the twelfth chapter. And we want to begin right there in verse 7. I want to encourage you again, to just move along with me using your Bible and making notes where you can or where you think it's applicable. Now moving to verse 7 in Revelation the twelfth chapter, It says here, ***"And war broke out in heaven: Michael and his angels fought with the dragon; and the dragon and his angels fought, but they did not prevail, nor was a place found for them in heaven any longer."***

Weapons of Our Warfare Section One

And I'm reading from the New King James, by the way.

> *"So the great dragon was cast out, that serpent of old, called the Devil and Satan, who deceives the whole world; he was cast to the earth, and his angels were cast out with him. Then I heard a loud voice saying in heaven, "Now salvation, and strength, and the kingdom of our God, and the power of His Christ have come, for the accuser of our brethren, who accused them before our God day and night, has been cast down. And they overcame him by the blood of the Lamb and by the word of their testimony, and they did not love their lives to the death. Therefore rejoice, O heavens, and you who dwell in them! Woe to the inhabitants of the earth and the sea! For the devil has come down to you, having great wrath, because he knows that he has a short time."*

Now I wanted to share that particular pericope of scripture, because I wanted to reinforce the fact that we are engaged in a spiritual war. And the spiritual war has a nature that's directed by an entity called Satan. Now again, we want to establish some things. Let's turn to Isaiah the fourteenth chapter. And again we are laying the foundation because there is no point in discussing the aspects of warfare or spiritual war without establishing the initiator or the instigator, who is Satan himself.

In Isaiah the 14th chapter, beginning in verse 12, it states, *"How you are fallen from heaven, O Lucifer…"* (Now we all know that Lucifer was Satan's name before he rebelled, and it says) *"…son of the morning! How you are cut down to the ground, You who weakened the nations!"*

Again identifying Satan's nature and the purpose for which he graduated to when he walked away from God's directive. Verse 13: *For you have said in your heart: "I will ascend into heaven, I will exalt my throne above the stars of God;"* "Stars," meaning the angels that God created. *"…I will also sit on the mount of the congregation On the farthest sides of the north."*

It says in verse 14, *"I will ascend above the heights of the clouds, I will be like the Most High."* He wanted to be like God. He wanted to usurp God's authority. *Yet you shall be brought down*...Says God... *to Sheol*...Other words, "hell" or "the pit","...*to the lowest depths of the Pit."*

Let's turn to Ezekiel 28, because again it describes behavior of a being that is not human, but supernatural. Ezekiel 28 beginning in verse 11, it says, *"Moreover the word of the LORD came to me, saying, "Son of man, take up a lamentation for the king of Tyre, and say to him, 'Thus says the Lord GOD."*

Relative to the King of Tyre, there will be a point in my lecture when we talk about territorial demons - - principalities who rule in physical figures. But as you listen you will soon become aware that we are not talking about a physical being here. It says, *"You were the seal of perfection, Full of wisdom and perfect in beauty.* "And that is no description of any human being that you and I know.

"You were in Eden, the Garden of God." So we know the King of Tyre was not in the Garden of Eden in the flesh. God is now speaking spiritually here. Let's continue in verse 13 of Ezekiel 28. *Every precious stone was your covering:...* And it names those stones. Going down to verse 14 it says, *...You were the anointed cherub who covers*; It becomes clearer and clearer who God is talking about. It says, *"I established you; You were on the holy mountain of God. You walked back and forth in the midst of fiery stones."*

No human being is capable of doing that. I know some people say "Well, I have seen individuals walk on hot coals." This was a great deal more than hot coals; this was fiery stones. It says, *"You were perfect in your ways from the day you were created, Till iniquity was found in you. By the abundance of your trading you became filled with violence within. And you sinned"*, So Satan sinned and his main sin was pride. And it says, *"Therefore I cast you as a profane thing out of the mountain of God."*

Which means the Kingdom of God, or the domain of God. *"And I destroyed you, O covering cherub, from the midst of the fiery stones."*

In other words, he was removed from his position of loftiness. His job was to be a light bringer to God's creation and he was Lucifer. That was his description. And as we have already noted in Isaiah 14 and Ezekiel 28, he was in a prominent position until he decided to rebel.

Second Point of Attack -Adam and Eve (9:51 T-3)

Now this happened long before the creation of Adam and Eve, but we want to bring this into a context in Genesis that few have truly understood, many have read, and too many have misunderstood.

Let's go to Genesis the first chapter, and in the first verse. It says here, *"In the beginning God created the heavens and the earth. "*Now in verse 2 it says, *"The earth was without form."*

I am reading New King James, but most translations or a lot of translations give the impression in reading the English translation or transliteration, as some may call it, that God created the Earth in chaos. That is not the case. When you look up that particular verse in the Hebrew (you should have a Hebrew Bible that has English alongside of it) then verse 2 reads, more in the context of *the earth became void and without form.* The Hebrew words there are *tohu* and *bohu,* which means it was a condition that became extant after the events in verse one. Now what happened between verses 1 and verses 2, and simply put, you may need to do extensive research on your own. But what happened was Isaiah 14 and Ezekiel 28.

See this was an event that happened after the creation of perfection because Satan was even created in perfection. Why would God create him in perfection as it says in Isaiah and Ezekiel and then create the Earth in imperfection? It became that way because of the battle that occurred in Isaiah 14 and Ezekiel 28. And when you do research you will find that in the Hebrew meaning of the words and when you understand the timeline, it becomes very clear. And, it is in perfect harmony with the text as you look at the Scriptures and the reality of Satan's impact, and what he should have been doing, and what he eventually did in the way of destruction and total chaos.

In John 10:10 it says, or in John the tenth chapter around verse 10 it says that the enemy comes but to kill, steal and destroy. And this is what he became between verses 1 and 2. What time expired between those two events? I have no idea. I just simply know that it occurred. Now, why is that important? Because as we move to Genesis the third chapter we can see that this conflict now that occurred pre-Adamic, is now brought to the Adamic realm or Adam's realm and Eve's realm. In Chapter 3 of Genesis we move from the heavenly battle as we have talked about in Revelation, Isaiah, Ezekiel, and Genesis 1, to where that battle is now reduced to the Earth.

And as we look at verse 1, it says, *Now the serpent ...* Who used to be Lucifer. *"Now the serpent was more cunning than any beast of the field which the Lord God had made."* And then again, that word <u>serpent</u> in Hebrew is "enchanter", is one of the meanings. But, there are a multiplicity of meanings. So when you think of serpent don't think of something just crawling but think of something with great persuasive power. And we are seeing here that the Lord God had made. *"And he said to the woman, [the serpent] Has God indeed said, 'You shall not eat of every tree of the garden?"*

Now, again, we see the enemy, Satan, now trying to bring his insurrection, his attitude of rebellion, sin to the realm of mankind. Because in verse 9 in Genesis the second chapter it talks about, "and out of the ground the Lord God made every tree grow." And it says, "In the midst of the garden there was the tree or trees that were good and pleasant and the tree of life was also in the midst" (I am paraphrasing) "of the Garden and the tree of the knowledge of good and evil."

Now it begins to talk about a river it goes down to verse 17 in Genesis the second chapter. Well, let's do verse 16. It says: *"And the Lord God commanded the man saying, of every tree of the garden you may freely eat, every tree but one. But of the tree..."* Verse 17,"*.... of the knowledge of good and evil you shall not eat, for in the day that you eat of it you shall surely die."*

Now, let's move back to Genesis 3 because you need to understand the subtlety in which the enemy operates, verse 1, Chapter 3.

"Now the serpent was more cunning than any beast of the field which the LORD God had made. And he said to the woman, "Has God indeed said, 'You shall not eat of every tree of the garden'?" And the woman said to the serpent, "We may eat the fruit of the trees of the garden; but of the fruit of the tree which is in the midst of the garden, God has said, 'You shall not eat of it, nor shall you touch it, lest you die."

Now in the instructions that we see that God gave to Adam we don't see any instructions about touching. Also, the tree of life was in the midst of the garden and according to Eve's response, she said that we could not eat of any tree that was in the midst of the garden. But it says the tree of life was also in the midst of the garden. Which meant that her response was not exactly correct. Now that goes to Adam's dissemination of information. But that is another piece of the lecture or this message. The key is here is that the enemy wanted to taint the instructions of God. *"Then the serpent said to the woman, You will not surely die.."*

Now God says "you will surely die" or "shall surely die." Notice the level of warfare and the subtlety. Satan only added two words, "you will not" or "not," if you just look at the true context. He added one word that took the truth and perverted it. And Satan goes on to say in verse 5, *For God knows that in the day you eat of it your eyes will be opened, and you will be like God, knowing good and evil." So when the woman saw that the tree was good for food... and a tree desirable to make one wise, she took*

Well, let me go back, because I may have missed a point here.

"So when the woman saw that the tree was good for food, that it was pleasant to the eyes, and a tree desirable to make one wise, she took of its fruit and ate. She also gave to her husband with her, and he ate."

Adam was present when this occurred. He was not far away. Because it does not say she ran to him and gave it to him. *"Then the eyes of both of them were opened, and they knew that they were naked; and they sewed fig leaves together and made themselves coverings."*

Now, obviously once this occurred they became somewhat concerned because they were naked. But in verse 25 of Genesis the second chapter; no, let us begin in verse 24 instead. It says, *"Therefore a man shall leave his father and mother and be joined to his wife, and they shall become one flesh. And they were both naked, the man and his wife, and were not ashamed."*

So soon as they heard Satan give his instruction counter to what God gave, they became ashamed of something they were not ashamed of prior to receiving instructions other than from God. And the point that I am trying to make here is that the demonic realm led by Satan has one function, and one function only; to disseminate misinformation to mankind in general, and to Christians specifically, in order to alter the purpose of God.

Now you need to recognize that, in altering the purpose of God, Satan attacked the throne of God first and led away a third of the angels. Then his second point was to attack God's human creation that was made in the image and likeness of God. So Satan could not usurp God so he went after God's likeness and image in the form of Adam and Eve.

So, the first attack was the heavens on God, the second point of attack was Adam and Eve, God's man and women created after God's likeness, and then of course the next natural progression of attack is the children.

Next Attack – The Children (22:14 T-4)

Let's turn to Genesis the fourth chapter. And you are familiar with the story with Abel and Cain and the offering. I just want to get right to the area where Satan makes his move. And we will begin at the middle part of the last part of verse 4 in Genesis the fourth chapter. And it says, ***And the LORD respected Abel and his offering, but He did not respect Cain and his offering. And Cain was very angry, and his countenance fell. So the LORD said to Cain,*** " God talked to Cain asking him a question. ***"Why are you angry? And why has your countenance fallen? If you do well, will you not be accepted?"***

Now a lot of people do not understand what happened with Cain and God. I will just simply submit this: The ground was cursed because of what Adam and Eve did. Cain gave an offering from cursed ground, rather than a lamb like Abel did. So God rejected and did not have respect for his offering. So God is telling him now in verse 7, ***"If you do well will you not be accepted? And if you do not do well, sin lies at the door."*** Satan, who is the original sinner, who put it into Adam and Eve and now being transferred in behavior to Cain. Now let's notice the second half of verse 7, and it states there: ***And its....*** That is sin's ***....desire is for you, but you should rule over it.*** In other words, God told Cain, You should exercise will power, through My help over the tendencies of anger that you have in you, because if you do not take control of it, it will take control of you.

Now let's take a look at verse 8. It begins with the words: ***Now Cain talked with Abel his brother; and it came to pass, when they were in the field, that Cain rose up against Abel his brother and killed him.***

So obviously Cain did not rule over that sin of anger, jealousy, a combination of those two, or a combination of another group of sins. He failed to rule over it and it led him to commit murder, bottom-line.

So again we see the spiritual conflict being perpetrated on man by Satan when he attacked the throne of God and failed to dethrone God but succeeded in confusing a third of the angels, it succeeded in confusing Adam and Eve, and it succeeded in leading Cain to murder.

So we have a solid foundation and this is not all the scriptural proof. This is just some basic foundational information to establish the fact biblically that spiritual warfare is a reality. It did not start in the New Testament; it is actually post- or pre- rather, Old Testament, and New Testament; it is pre-creation of Adam and Eve; and has been brought into the realm of human beings which includes us who are impacted by emotions, directives, inclinations, feelings, tendencies, urges, impulses that are instigated and whispered via Satan and his kingdom. And we have witnessed the impact that it had on our initial parents and on our initial siblings, Cain and Abel.

Old Testament Demonic Impact or Influence (27:38 T-5)

But now we want to talk about just briefly some Old Testament impacts or situations or scenarios where Satan manifested himself into the affairs of men and leaders of God and caused some conflict, confusion, rebellion and sin.

An Episode with David (28:15)

Let's turn to I Chronicles 21. We want to turn to I Chronicles 21 and this is under the Old Testament Demonic Impact or Influence. Now let's take a look at verse 1 in I Chronicles 21. It's says, ***Now Satan stood up against Israel and moved David to number Israel.*** In other words, my brothers and sisters, Satan influenced David to number Israel.

Now we know that is a problem because anytime Satan influences anybody, it is a problem. Let's look at verse 7 in the same chapter of I Chronicles 21. It says there, ***And God was displeased with this thing; therefore He struck Israel. So David said to God, "I have sinned greatly, because I have done this thing;***

So David realized and knew that he was doing something God did not want him to do. But Satan stood up against the nation of Israel and influenced the leadership to create a problem that caused the whole nation or should I say, the whole household, a problem. Again, establishing that Satan does have impact and tries to interject himself into the plan of God to alter those who have been given direction, to alter that direction, and to alter that individual into doing something God has not directed them to do. Again, it does not end there.

An Episode with Job (30:33 T-6)

Let's turn to Job. Again, where there is another example of Satan having impact in the realm of man very directly. The supernatural impacting the natural and very specifically, in the realm of man. Let's turn to Job the 1st chapter and let's begin in verse 6. It says, ***Now there was a day when the sons of God came to present themselves before the LORD, and Satan also came among them.*** So the angels, who are also called the sons of God via creation not sons of God through adoption. It says here in verse 7: ***And the LORD said to Satan, "From where do you come?" So Satan answered the LORD and said, "From going to and fro on the earth, and from walking back and forth on it." Then the LORD said to Satan, "Have you considered My servant Job,"***

So you need to understand something, God will sometimes point you out to Satan in order to see where you are. It says, ***"Have you considered My servant Job, that there is none like him on the earth, a blameless and upright man, one who fears God and shuns evil?" So Satan answered the LORD and said, "Does Job fear God for nothing? Have You not made a hedge around him, around his household, and around all that he has on every side? You have blessed the work of his hands, and his possessions have increased in the land.***

But Satan says to God in verse 11:

> *'But now, stretch out Your hand and touch all that he has, and he will surely curse You to Your face! And the L*ORD* said to Satan, Behold, all that he has is in your power; only do not lay a hand on his person." So Satan went out from the presence of the L*ORD*."*

And now we can go to verses 13 and 14. Read what happened. My point is this, that spiritual warfare is real. And sometimes God wants to know where you stand. What you need to understand is Satan has no power except for what God allows. And he has no influence over you except what you give him. What am I saying? I am saying that even though God allowed Satan to attack Job, Job still had the power over what he said and did. Because Satan said, "If you remove your hedge he will curse you to your face." So Satan was counting on whatever he did forcing Job into anti-God or anti-Christ behavior. So again, we are looking at a level of warfare where Satan is trying to pull man off of his purpose, and that purpose is defined by God.

Leviathan (34:58)

Now, I just want to move again in the book of Job to Job 41, where, in the middle of everything that Job is experiencing, there is a chapter, chapter 41, that seems to be out of place, but it isn't. It is exactly where it needs to be, because Job 41 does not talk about a sea creature as some have interpreted as describing. And I will just simply point you to verse 34. It will clear that misnomer up. In verse 34 of chapter 41 of Job, it says, *"He...* Talking about Leviathan. *He beholds every high thing ;He is king over all the children of pride."*

That does not describe the level of power or influence of some giant fish in the ocean. Leviathan is a very powerful demon of pride. And the reason God put chapter 41 here was to help us to understand that Job was having an issue with pride that was supernatural and not physical. Because if you go into chapter 42 it says, ***"Then Job answered the L*ORD *and said: I know that You can do everything, And that no purpose...", "*** In the King James it says *"that no thought can be withheld from You."* And Job was acknowledging, "Lord, I know the issue was that You knew what I was thinking and although my behavior was righteous and all these other things were righteous, there was a sin of pride in me that You wanted me to recognize and repent of." As we move on in the second half of verse 3 in chapter 42 it says, ***"Therefore I have uttered what I did not understand, Things too wonderful for me, which I did not know."*** Then he goes on to say, ***"I have heard of You by the hearing of the ear, now my eye sees You.*** Job's spiritual eyes were opened up. And in verse 6 he says, **Therefore I abhor myself, repent in dust and ashes."**

So Job repented; once God allowed a trial to cause him to focus. But Job did what Cain did not do. After much anguish he was able to stay with God's instructions and see what it was that he needed to change in his life and he took rule and took charge over it, and did not allow it to rule over him, and God restored him after he acknowledged his sin and repented of it. So that is the key, to be able to do in spiritual warfare what Job did at the end, and that is to acknowledge, recognize and repent of anything that's contrary to the Word of God.

New Testament Demonic Impact or Influence (39:33 T-7)

Now, let's move to the New Testament and let's look at some key scriptures that will surprise some of you, but many of you will recognize this as part of your spiritual walk. Let's turn to Luke, the tenth chapter and we want to look at how the demonic manifested itself or how Christ in one circumstance addressed it. Many may say "Demons don't exist." I will say that if Christ acknowledges something then it does exist. Luke 10, verse 17, the Gospel of Luke, chapter 10, verse 17 and it says, ***"Then the seventy returned with joy, saying, "Lord, even the demons are subject to us in Your name."***

Now at that point Christ would have corrected them if demons did not exist. As He corrected Peter when Christ was explaining what had to happen to Him and Peter said, "No, it's not." And Christ told Peter, "***Get behind me Satan.*** " He corrected him. But in contrast, He did not correct any of the seventy when they reported on demons being subject to them in His name. And as we look at verse 18 and He said to them, ***I saw Satan fall like lightning from heaven.***

This is proof emphatically, as far as I am concerned, scripturally based, out of the mouth of Jesus Himself, that demons and Satan do exist. The seventy were talking about how the demons are subject to them, because of the name of Christ and His response was not that, "You are mistaken," but that, "***I saw Satan fall like lightening from Heaven.***" Now, but listen to verse 19, Christ goes on to further solidify the existence of the demonic realm and their influence over mankind by saying,

Behold, I give you the authority to trample on serpents and scorpions, and over all the power of the enemy, and nothing shall by any means hurt you. And all the power of the enemy is: cancer, high blood pressure, poor living conditions, poverty, joblessness, anguish, depression. God has given us power over the enemy who is Satan and those who work for him in the demonic realm. God would not waste time giving you power over something that does not exist. I mean, God is not ignorant. I think that's an understatement, and I might just be at this point having a little fun with this. But I think it's pretty clear.

<u>Caution (43:10)</u>

But let's move on, because there is an important key here, and I want to also at this point issue a caution. Because in many movements that deal in deliverance or inner healing, charismatic movements and other movements, and other denominations when they get involved and acknowledge this activity, there is a degree of supremacy and an attitude of superiority that sometimes comes over individuals who understand this to a degree. But listen at the caution that our Wonderful Savior Jesus Christ with His great degree of balance, or should I say, His perfection of balance, gives after He articulates 17, 18, and 19 of Luke 10. Listen to what He says, *Nevertheless...*In verse 20 *...do not rejoice...*Be prideful, boast, be arrogant, puffed up, or exalt yourself, and I am adding some things there around the word "rejoice." *... that the spirits are subject to you,* So don't get all bent out of shape about that. He says,*... but rather rejoice...*Be elated, boastful.*...because your names are written in heaven."*

So He says your focus on the Kingdom of God is more important than controlling, or ruling, or directing or battling the demonic realm from a perspective of pride and just for the sheer purpose of engagement. He gave us the power to be able to set people free. That's the whole purpose for having power over the spiritual realm in the arena of spiritual warfare.

Luke 4:18-19 (45:39)

Now let's turn to Luke the fourth chapter because it is important that you understand Luke 4:18, 19. It says here: *The Spirit of the LORD is upon Me, Because He has anointed Me To preach the gospel to the poor; He has sent Me to heal the brokenhearted, To proclaim liberty to the captives And recovery of sight to the blind, To set at liberty those who are oppressed; To proclaim the acceptable year of the LORD."*

In other words - deliverance and healing. Christ says He was anointed to do that and as He brings us into His disciple arena then He empowers us to do the same. There is a spiritual realm that has impact on mankind.

Luke 4:31 – 34 (46:41)

Now let's begin to see some examples of a direct demon activity in again Luke the fourth chapter, we want to go to verse 31, and it says here, *Then He went down to Capernaum, a city of*

Galilee, and was teaching them on the Sabbaths; and they were astonished at His teaching, for His word was with authority.

Christ was not a wimp and it says *Now* in verse 33 *"Now in the synagogue…"* And you know our churches are nothing but modern-day synagogues. I am not talking about in the way that worship was conducted in the Jewish tradition. I'm talking about as a matter of fact relative to a place of worship. It says, *"Now in the synagogue there was a man who had a spirit of an unclean demon. And he cried out with a loud voice."*

We do have demonized people in our churches. It doesn't matter if we believe it or not, whether or not we accept it. And in verse 34 it says, and the demon said, *"Let us alone! What have we to do with You, Jesus of Nazareth?"* So that's one example of demons being in a religious scenario where religious worship is taking place and there is demons sitting up in that environment and were manifest when the Word showed up in the form of Jesus Christ.

Impacts Men and Women (48:38)

But that's not the only example; let's turn to Luke the 8th chapter. Again, we are laying the foundation in the New Testament. And we want to go to verse 1, and it says, *Now it came to pass,* In Luke 8:1 *Afterward, that He went through every city and village, preaching and bringing the glad tidings of the kingdom of God. And the twelve were with Him, and certain women who had been healed of evil spirits and infirmities--Mary called Magdalene, out of whom had come seven demons.* So we see that men can be impacted by demons and women can be impacted by demons.

Multiple Possession (49:32 T-8)

Also, let's look at verse 26 in the same chapter of Luke and we can see a scenario of multiple demon possession. It says, *Then they sailed to the country of the Gadarenes, which is opposite Galilee. And when He stepped out on the land, there met Him a certain man from the city who had demons for a long time. And he wore no clothes, nor did he live in a house but in the tombs.* So here is someone who you may call homeless who had been infected and controlled by demons. Again Christ confronted it.

Impacts Children, Also (50:32)

Now let's look at Luke 9 because here we see where demons can also impact children. In verse 37 it says, *Now it happened on the next day, when they had come down from the mountain, that a great multitude met Him. a man from the multitude cried out, saying, "Teacher, I implore You, look on my son, for he is my only child. And behold, a spirit seizes him, and he suddenly cries out; it convulses him so that he foams at the mouth; and it departs from him with great difficulty, bruising him. So I implored Your disciples to cast it out, but they could not."* Then Jesus had some dialog with the man about bearing with the generation. *And as he was still coming, the demon threw him down* ...When the young man was coming in verse 42,...*and convulsed him. Then Jesus rebuked the unclean spirit, healed the child, and gave him back to his father.* I just wanted to lay a preliminary foundation, so you would understand that we are just not "beating the air" here. We are just not hallucinating and trying to articulate things that are not scripturally sound.

Apostle Paul (52:28 T9)

But let's move on to the Apostle Paul because he had a few things to say about spiritual warfare and some of the things that we need to be aware of in our Christian walk, in order to be protected and aware.

Ephesians 6:10 -14

Let's turn to Ephesians the sixth chapter and we are going to begin at verse 10, because many believe that Christians cannot be demonized and/or possessed. But let's look at what Paul says, and he is speaking primarily to the Christian body. *"**Finally, my brethren, be strong in the Lord and in the power of His might.**"*

So that opening comment in verse 10 is a comment directed toward Christians. It says in verse 11,

Put on the whole armor of God, that you may be able to stand against the wiles of the devil. For we do not wrestle against flesh and blood, but against principalities, against powers, against the rulers of the darkness of this age, against spiritual hosts of wickedness in the heavenly places. Therefore take up the whole armor of God, that you may be able to withstand in the evil day, and having done all, to stand. Stand therefore, having girded your waist with truth.

And I won't read any further. My point is, is that we as Christians have to be prepared to do battle with Satan because we can be affected and infected.

II Corinthians 10: 3-5 (54:41)

Let's turn to II Corinthians the tenth chapter, and again we see where Paul is giving some instructions relative to spiritual warfare to Christians dealing with the spiritual realm, and here he identifies it as a stronghold. Let's move to verse 3, and we see here it says, **For though we walk in the flesh, we do not war according to the flesh.**

Reiterating a statement he made in Ephesians or vice versa. In verse 4:

"For the weapons of our warfare are not carnal but mighty in God for pulling down strongholds, casting down arguments and every high thing that exalts itself against the knowledge of God, bringing every thought into captivity to the obedience of Christ."

So it has to do with mental activity and what we think. It is a spiritual activity, and what we think is always being impacted by the enemy. That's why God said what He said to Cain.

II Corinthians 11:13– 15 (56:13)

Let's move over now to the eleventh chapter of II Corinthians and let's focus here on verse 13. It says, *For such are false apostles, deceitful workers, transforming themselves into apostles of Christ.*

Now we are breaking into a thought here in chapter 11. Paul is trying to make a point about deception, and as we move to verse 14. And he says, *And no wonder! For Satan himself transforms himself into an angel of light.*

Because he used to be the Light Bringer so he can make that false transition. In verse 15 it says, *"Therefore it is no great thing if his ministers also transform themselves into ministers of righteousness, whose end will be according to their works."* So Satan just doesn't work with demons in the spirit realm. He also can influence individuals who even wear the title of minister to do what he wants done.

I Timothy 4:1- 2 (57:38)

Let's move to I Timothy 4, again we are still kind of laying the foundation but also taking that opportunity in laying the foundation to impart some information. Let's move to I Timothy the 4th chapter and start with verse 1. It says there, *Now the Spirit expressly says that in latter times some will depart from the faith, giving heed to deceiving spirits and doctrines of demons, speaking lies in hypocrisy, having their own conscience seared with a hot iron.* So Paul is warning Christians do not be seduced by demons.

Acts 8: 1–7 (58:35)

Now, let's turn to Acts, again just establishing some things so we can begin to actually discuss this arena without a whole lot of debate about the reality of this arena, and making sure that there is a Biblical foundation laid in respect to spiritual warfare. That's Acts the 8th chapter beginning in verse 4, it says, **Therefore those who were scattered went everywhere preaching the word**.

And this is after some persecution on the Church. Let's focus on verse 5 now, and it says, **Then Philip went down to the city of Samaria and preached Christ to them. And the multitudes with one accord heeded the things spoken by Philip, hearing and seeing the miracles which he did.** Verse 7 **For unclean spirits, crying with a loud voice, came out of many who were possessed; and many who were paralyzed and lame were healed. And there was great joy in that city.**

So the word there "possessed" is really in the Greek "demonized" or "who have demons", because again possession and demonization are degrees of attack. But, we won't spend a lot of time on that. I just simply want to say that Satan can possess and enter into individuals.

I want to end this particular segment or this area of discussion with John 13:27, that's John 13:27. Now I want to take just a couple of seconds here to point out that Christ was establishing something. He was engaged with the disciples. It was kind of their last real meal together before "the betrayal", and the main character or the main character of focus in verse 27 is Judas. So as we break into the context of this text then we will know and understand as we read it we realize that Christ is identifying something here and Satan is also identifying something here. So in verse 27 of John 13 we read, **"Now after the piece of bread, Satan entered him. Then Jesus said to him, "What you do, do quickly."**

Speaking to Judas. *But no one at the table knew for what reason He said this to him.* They had no idea that Judas was about to betray Jesus Christ after Satan had entered him.

Conclusion (62:12 T-10)

So, as we move to the conclusion of this section of the lecture, I just want you to understand that we have laid a foundation, we have demonstrated scripturally in the Old as well as the New Testament that Satan and demons do exist. They do have access to us, non-Christians, as well as Christians, and we want to understand that the focus on spiritual warfare that was articulated by Apostle Paul and the other apostles is a reality that we must address in the body of Christ.

Now as we conclude this particular segment of the lecture, I just want to give a few more scriptures relative to demonization of Christians. You know you still can sin after being baptized and you still can sin after receiving the Holy Spirit. And sin makes you vulnerable to demonization. Now let's turn to Acts the 8th chapter, and let's look at verse 9. And there it states,

"But there was a certain man called Simon, who previously practiced sorcery in the city and astonished the people of Samaria, claiming that he was someone great," Verse 10, *"to whom they all gave heed, from the least to the greatest, saying, This man is the great power of God. And they heeded him because he had astonished them with his sorceries for a long time. But when they believed Philip as he preached the things concerning the kingdom of God and the name of Jesus Christ, both men and women were baptized. Then Simon himself also believed; and when he was baptized he continued with Philip, and was amazed, seeing the miracles and signs which were done."*

So here we have what they normally called this individual in history Simon Magus, but here we have an individual who was baptized. Now let's look at verse 14. It says,

> *"Now when the apostles who were at Jerusalem heard that Samaria had received the word of God, they sent Peter and John to them"* Verse 15, *"who, when they had come down, prayed for them that they might receive the Holy Spirit. For as yet* **(in verse 16)** *He had fallen upon none of them. They had only been baptized in the name of the Lord Jesus. Then they laid hands on them, and they received the Holy Spirit. And when Simon saw that through the laying on of the apostles' hands the Holy Spirit was given, he offered them money, saying, Give me this power also, that anyone on whom I lay hands may receive the Holy Spirit."*

Now this is an attitude that was still pervasive in this man, after he had been baptized, after he had confessed and repented of his so-called sorcery. Verse 20,

> *"But Peter said to him, Your money perish with you, because you thought that the gift of God could be purchased with money! You have neither part nor portion in this matter, for your heart is not right in the sight of God. Repent therefore of this your wickedness, and pray God if perhaps the thought of your heart may be forgiven you."*

The bottom line here is that even after you have been baptized and received the Holy Spirit, you can have thoughts and motives that are not godly, that open you up to influences, past influences - - in Simon's case, manipulating and being deceitful, wanting to buy the power to be able to impart the Holy Spirit through the laying on of hands. Now, that's just one example. We can all cite personal examples in our own lives and we can all identify examples we have observed in the lives of others.

This concludes our foundational information relative to the overall message, *"**Weapons of Our Warfare**."* We will continue to go into detail in the next CD, be sure to pick it up! May God bless you for listening and guide you and give you the strength you need to be able to comprehend, understand and to implement His words in your life.

Weapons of Our Warfare Section One

Weapons of Our Warfare Section Two

Weapons of Our Warfare Section Two

Weapons of Our Warfare Section Two

Table of Contents

Lecture Section Two 28
    Introduction T-1..31
    Point of Attack:
    Adam and Eve/Marriage T-2........................31
    Jesus Christ, the Second Adam T-3 36
    Rebellion is Paramount to Witchcraft T-4 ...36
    Advice to Husband and Wives T-5................38
        Advice to Singles 40
    Biblical Reference to Drug Use T-6..............45
    Spiritual STDs T-7 46
    Adam, Christ, Eve and the Church
    -The Relationship T-8.....................................48
    The Mind of Christ T-9 51
        Christ's Mission..............................51
        The Weapons of Our Warfare........52
        Subduing the Strongman 53
    Staying Free T-10...54

Weapons of Our Warfare Section Two

Introduction (T-1)

Amen and Amen.

This is Dr. Maddox again. And of course if you've listened to the first segment of this lecture, you know that we're dealing with the weapons of our warfare and we've covered some foundational information. Now we want to move into some areas which I'll call points of attack, points of attack relative to how Satan engages us in the human realm.

Point of Attack: Adam and Eve/Marriage (0:34 T-2)

Let's turn to Genesis the 1st chapter and we want to begin here in verse 26. It says here:

"Then God said, "Let Us make man in Our image, according to Our likeness; let them have dominion over the fish of the sea, over the birds of the air, and over the cattle, over all the earth and over every creeping thing that creeps on the earth. So God created man in His own image; in the image of God He created him; male and female He created them."

Now let's go to Genesis the 2nd chapter. And let's land in verse 18 and I am reading from the New King James and also I want to take this opportunity to encourage you to get your Bibles, get something to write with and something to write on. Genesis the 2nd chapter, verse 18: *"And the LORD God said, It is not good that man should be alone; I will make him a helper comparable to him."*

Someone suitable, in other words. And verse 19, it says:

"Out of the ground the LORD God formed every beast of the field and every bird of the air, and brought them to Adam to see what he would call them. And whatever Adam called each living creature, that was its

name. So Adam gave names to all cattle, to the birds of the air, and to every beast of the field. But for Adam there was not found a helper comparable to him."

Or compatible, to use another term. Genesis, the 2nd chapter, verse 21:

"And the LORD God caused a deep sleep to fall on Adam, and he slept; and He took one of his ribs, and closed up the flesh in its place. Then the rib which the LORD God had taken from man He made into a woman, and He brought her to the man. And Adam said: This is now bone of my bones And flesh of my flesh; She shall be called Woman, Because she was taken out of Man. Therefore a man shall leave his father and mother and be joined to his wife, and they shall become one flesh."

Now I wanted to establish this to show that Adam and Eve were compatible, comparable and equal in the context of being in the likeness and the image of God although there was order as it is order in the Trinity: God, the Father, Son and the Holy Spirit. As in the human realm, there is order: the man, and the woman, and the children. But it doesn't mean that there is not cooperation, and that there should be domination or abuse. And being subject does not mean you are humiliated or dehumanized. So I wanted to make sure that we established that.

Now let's go to Ephesians the 5th chapter. And I just want to read that area of Scripture that focuses on marriage, in the context of the church and Jesus Christ. But I just want to begin here in verse 22. It says: *"Wives, submit to your own husbands, as to the Lord."* And verse 23 it says: *"For the husband is head of the wife, as also Christ is head of the church; and He is the Savior of the body."* We're talking about roles and responsibilities. Let's go to verse 24:

"Therefore, just as the church is subject to Christ, so let the wives be to their own husbands in everything. Husbands, love your wives, just as Christ also loved the

church and gave Himself for her, that He might sanctify and cleanse her with the washing of water by the word."

Basically, husbands are to love their wives through teaching them the Word of God and being an example of Christ to them in their lives. Now that doesn't sound like an abusive, totalitarian situation of domination. It sounds like a loving environment and that's the way God created it to be.

But when that does not occur unfortunately Satan was able to get in and begin to pervert and twist. Now, none of us are really sure what happened that caused Eve to be susceptible to Satan's suggestion, but we can infer based on human behavior that she was unhappy. Satan deduced it and that's when he made his move.

Even in the natural, when couples are having problems in their relationships, it is detectable and you will have individuals, whether it be male or female, who can read the stress, see the behavior and begin to make moves. You have men who can see that women may be having difficulty in their relationships and will try to lure them into an illicit, fornicative or adulterous relationship. The same way with women who may see men who are married having difficulties in their marriage providing that understanding, that some claim that is not received from their wives. All I am saying is there are obvious behavior factors. So when we look at verse 8 and 9 in Genesis the 2nd chapter, and we look at what God did relative to planting of the garden and making certain trees available and putting one on restriction. And then when we go to Genesis the 3rd chapter and we look at what occurred there, in verse 1: *"Now the serpent was more cunning than any beast of the field."* Now as we move to verse 2: *And the woman said to the serpent...."*

And the serpent approached the woman. Just like most men would approach a woman that they believe to be in a condition of vulnerability and open to suggestion. Because we can assume from what's in the text that there were some issues. Now let's move to verse 11 and I want to substantiate something here. Because you're all familiar with the story. And I am not going to take time to read all of that now. What I want to focus on is that a point of attack is to attack the marriage and the relationship between a man and a woman. And look what God said to Adam in verse 11: *"And He said, Who told you that you were naked? Have you eaten from the tree of which I commanded you that you should not eat?"*

And He commanded him in Genesis, the 2nd chapter. Now in verse 12 it says: *"Then the man said,"* Now listen to this: *"Then the man said, "The woman whom You gave to be with me, she gave me of the tree, and I ate."*

First of all, Adam blamed God. He said the woman you gave me, so it's your fault, then it's her fault. Adam had an attitude, here. An attitude that manifested and revealed that there were some issues. Because Adam and Eve were not in the context of Ephesians the 5th chapter and we have to believe that God gave them the instructions they needed to have a happy, balanced marriage. And we have to recognize that Satan did not make his first intrusion to create problems in this relationship as we see in Genesis the 3rd chapter. What we see in Genesis the 3rd chapter is the culmination of subtle effort and what we would call a "blitz" on the football field. Where Satan knew that their scenario had gotten to the point where Adam, even though he heard what he was saying to Eve, because he was there, that he would not intervene for whatever reason and not only not intervene, partake of and then as we see in verse 12, even blame God.

So the first point of attack is to create division in the family between the man and woman, create doubt in their minds about what God has said and then plant information that is not from God and persuade people to disobey God under the guise of being better off than you were. And when you go back up and you look at verse 3. And it says here: ..."*but of the fruit of the tree which is in the midst of the garden".* This is what Eve is saying we're not supposed to eat. And then Satan says in verse 5, "Oh, God knows that you're going to be as great as He is when you do it."

And in verse 6 it says: *"So when the woman saw that the tree was good for food, that it was pleasant to the eyes, and a tree desirable to make one wise, she took..."* So it's the lusts of the eyes, the lusts of the flesh and the pride of life, the same tactic he used on Jesus Christ to [try to] lure Him into disobedience. And once he was able to do that [to Adam] that was a form of worship. So we need to understand that submission and loving one another will safeguard us from this type of demonic intrusion, but when we don't, we open ourselves up to strategies that are created in the realm of demonic influence. And eventually leading us to sin, demonization and eventually death.

Now you can present a lot of arguments about what may have happened here. From a man's perspective it is always given from a pro-male perspective that Eve made the mistake, and Adam didn't. That Eve messed up and Adam didn't.

Let's turn to I Timothy. Because I think part of the problem here with Adam and Eve was rejection on somebody's part. But I think we need to understand that part of what Satan has been able to do is to cause the male gender to view this as entirely an Eve issue. And it is not entirely an Eve issue. It's an Adam and Eve issue. We need to recognize that in verse 14 of 1 Timothy, the second chapter, we need to understand what it says here. It says: ***"And Adam was not deceived, but the woman being deceived, fell into transgression"***.

Now I am going to pose a question, and you need to answer it: If Adam wasn't deceived and what Eve did was based on being deceived by Satan, then why did Adam disobey a direct command from God? If you are not deceived, then you consciously make a decision. So Adam was in a state of rebellion and Eve was in a state of deception. Which makes them partners in the sin.

Read that Scripture for yourself. Read it in the Greek. No matter how you slice it, if there is deception then there is a decision made based on information and understanding, which concludes into rebellion.

Let's turn to I Samuel 15 and I want to make a point here. Now many theologians and some clergymen will dispute this with their last breath because there is a mindset to protect the integrity of

Adam, right or wrong. My focus is to protect the integrity of the Scripture. And when God says you are not deceived, then I tend to believe that God knows what He's talking about. And if you are not deceived then the only thing left is, you made an informed decision. And that is tantamount to rebellion when you know. And rebellion, let's point out what rebellion is. Because then you can understand why what occurred in the Garden was so paramount.

Jesus Christ, the Second Adam (18:20 T-3)

Now I just want to draw your attention, quickly, to I Corinthians 15, verses 20-28. And in that particular text it talks about Adam. And it also talks about Christ. It talks about sin coming in through Adam. But also deliverance coming in through Christ. In fact, it identifies Christ as the second Adam. Now I need to point out to you that that particular statement is not made between the verses 20 and 28 of I Corinthians 15. But let me bring your focus to verse 45 of I Corinthians 15. And it says here:

And so it is written, "The first man Adam became a living being. The last Adam became a life-giving spirit. However, the spiritual is not first, but the natural, and afterward the spiritual. The first man was of the earth, made of dust; the second Man is the Lord from heaven."

So that's where I am able to scripturally make the statement that Christ is the second Adam. Amen. Now I started off this particular piece of dialog with talking about rebellion and I deviated just a little bit in I Corinthians 15, but what we need to do now is get back to what rebellion is and we can do that now as we move forward.

Rebellion is Paramount to Witchcraft (20:00 T-4)

Let's move to I Samuel 15 and verse 23: And if you read the whole chapter you'll see that Saul did a bunch of things that he wasn't told to do and tried to justify them before God. And Samuel finally told him in verse 23:

> *"For rebellion is as the sin of witchcraft, And stubbornness is as iniquity and idolatry. Because you have rejected the word of the LORD, also has rejected you from being king."*

So the point is, there was a rejection of God's instruction which led to Adam and Eve being escorted out of the Garden. And I just want to make an interesting point here. Some of you who will be listening to this have children who are of age who don't want to obey God but want to live in your house. God, The Original Parent, when Adam and Even disobeyed the rules of the house, He put 'them out. And He not only put them out, He put an angel and a flaming sword to keep them from getting back in. That didn't mean He did not care for them. He provided them with clothes and He was concerned for them. But they could not stay in His house, the Garden of Eden, in a state of rebellion. And we need to understand that. Because a state of rebellion is paramount to witchcraft, witchcraft is paramount to demonization or demon activity. Again, a point of attack. If Satan can get you off point with the Word of God, then he can lure you into a level of confusion.

In II Corinthians the 11th chapter: beginning in verse 1, it says: *"Oh, that you would bear with me in a little folly—and indeed you do bear with me."* And Paul is getting ready to describe some things. He is correcting the Church here, the body of Christ. He says:

> *"For I am jealous for you with godly jealousy. For I have betrothed you to one husband, that I may present you as a chaste virgin to Christ. But I fear, lest somehow, as the serpent deceived Eve by his craftiness, so your minds may be corrupted from the simplicity that is in Christ. For if he who comes preaches..."*

In other words, if someone comes and they're preaching *"...another Jesus whom we have not preached, or if you receive a different spirit which you have not received, or a different gospel which you have not accepted—you may well put up with it!"*

In other words, Paul says some of you are putting up with this. And notice he is talking about another spirit other than the one that you have received. Again evidence that you can be a Christian and end up with a spirit you shouldn't have. Also again pointing out that through craftiness Eve was deceived. But Adam was not deceived through craftiness. He made a decision that lead to rebellion.

So again the first point of attack: Man must be in his place in the home as head operating under Christ, being directed by the Holy Spirit and subject to the call of the Father in order to provide the kind of loving environment that a wife would enjoy and not only enjoy, work to be submissive in. Because if that is not the case, then the first level of corruption is going to be with the man and the woman, the husband and the wife.

Advice to Husbands and Wives (24:50 T-5)

Now I want to share a word of advice out of the Scripture to the man and woman, and this is to husbands and wives. If you, by the way, are living together and you're not married, you're living in sin and none of this advice will benefit you. Sin is sin and you cannot be benefited by the Word of God, living in sin. Now let me clarify that to say this: if you're living in fornication, you're not going to receive the blessings of marriage in fornication, if you're committing adultery you're not going to receive the blessings of marriage, living in adultery. If you're living in homosexuality or lesbianism you're not going to receive the blessings of a God- ordained relationship, man and woman, living in that condition. So I just want to make sure that there is no misunderstanding. I don't want anybody claiming anything from this that I did not say. That's why I'm very clear in what I am saying.

Now let's turn to I Peter, and we want to go to the 3rd chapter, and we just want to read something here in verse 1: **"Likewise, be submissive to your own husbands, that even if** *some do not obey the word, they, without a word, may be won by the conduct of their wives."* In order words, women who are submissive can win an unconverted husband. It says:"*...when they observe your chaste conduct accompanied by fear."* Fear of God, not fear of them.

"Do not let your adornment be merely outward— arranging the hair, wearing gold, or putting on fine apparel..." It doesn't mean that you shouldn't look nice. What it means that your focus in looking nice shouldn't be to attract undue attention. *"...rather let it be the hidden person of the heart,.."*, what goes on within,*..."with the incorruptible beauty of a gentle and quiet spirit, which is very precious in the sight of God.*

Verse 6: *"For in this manner, in former times, the holy women who trusted in God also adorned themselves, being submissive to their own husbands."* That was verse 5, rather, and it says in verse 6:"...*as Sarah obeyed Abraham, calling him lord, whose daughters you are if you do good and are not afraid with any terror. Husbands, likewise, dwell with them with understanding"* Dwelling with them, with your wives. *"...giving honor to the wife, as to the weaker vessel..."* physically, and I'm adding that, because I don't believe it is mentally, spiritually, socially or any other way. I think a man's stature is created and his frame and his muscle structure was created to be stronger than a woman's. It says "vessel" as far as container and it says: *"...and as being heirs together of the grace of life, that your prayers may not be hindered."*

In other words, both of your prayers are going to be hindered if you don't have that focus. I want to also draw your attention to Ephesians 5:15-21, and I Corinthians 7:1-24. I think you should take time to read those verses.

But let's turn to Colossians the 3rd chapter. Because we want to look at another set of instructions that I think may be helpful in understanding the context of how we should be functioning in order to keep the enemy from invading our homes.

That's Colossians 3:18. And it says, again:

> *"Wives, submit to your own husbands, as is fitting in the Lord. Husbands, love your wives and do not be bitter toward them. Children, obey your parents in all things, for this is well pleasing to the Lord. Fathers, do not provoke your children, lest they become discouraged. Bondservants,"*

It's talking here:

> *"... obey in all things your masters according to the flesh, not with eye service, as men-pleasers, but in sincerity of heart, fearing God. And whatever you do, do it heartily, as to the Lord and not to men, knowing that from the Lord you will receive the reward of the inheritance; for you serve the Lord Christ."*

As we move to verse 25. We just read verses 23 and 24. Verse 25: *"But he who does wrong will be repaid for what he has done, and there is no partiality."*

The bottom line here is that God is saying that if you do not obey His instructions, for marriage and family there will be consequences because the enemy will find an inroad into your family and create issues of a demonic nature coupled with our own nature and pervert what it is that God initially intended in the Garden of Eden. So we need to recognize that.

Advice to Singles (31:58)

Now I want to just speak to the single people for one moment, here. In I Corinthians the 7th chapter. And we want to begin in verse 29:

> *"But this I say, brethren, the time is short, so that from now on even those who have wives should be as*

though they had none, those who weep as though they did not weep, those who rejoice as though they did not rejoice, those who buy as though they did not possess, and those who use this world as not misusing it. For the form of this world is passing away. But I want you to be without care. He who is unmarried cares for the things of the Lord—how he may please the Lord. But he who is married cares about the things of the world—how he may please his wife. There is a difference between a wife and a virgin. The unmarried woman cares about the things of the Lord, that she may be holy both in body and in spirit. But she who is married cares about the things of the world—how she may please her husband. And this I say for your own profit, not that I may put a leash on you, but for what is proper, and that you may serve the Lord without distraction. But if any man thinks he is behaving improperly toward his virgin, if she is past the flower of youth, and thus it must be, let him do what he wishes. He does not sin; let them marry."

"Nevertheless he who stands steadfast in his heart, having no necessity, but has power over his own will, and has so determined in his heart that he will keep his virgin, does well. So then he who gives her in marriage does well, but he who does not give her in marriage does better. A wife is bound by law as long as her husband lives; but if her husband dies..." Or if he dies:"*...she is at liberty to be married to whom she wishes, only in the Lord. But she is happier if she remains as she is, according to my judgment—and I think I also have the Spirit of God."*

And my point here, and the point that Paul is trying to make, is that in perilous times, it may be better not to seek to get married. But if you're going to seek to get married, then it is better to marry someone in the faith. And it is better to make sure that you have a relationship with God.

So single people, just don't jump up because someone is in church and assume they have a relationship with God. You better make sure. You seek counsel that you talk to your pastor, and other wise leaders, get the guidance you need. Don't get trapped into this dating, this western mentality of what dating is, which includes sex, necking and other things that are contrary to the context of the Word of God.

And Paul is speaking in urgency because he believed Christ was coming back. There was a great deal of persecution on the Church. So he spoke with urgency. I'm not going to speak with the same degree of urgency, right now. But I will say this. It's important that you know that the person you are talking about marrying has a solid relationship with Christ.

And if you are involved in any sexual activity prior to marriage with someone you want to marry, you've already started the relationship with a taintedness that is going to follow you into the marriage unless you repent before God because God can restore you both.

Now let's talk a little bit about sexual context and what I mean by sexual context is the proper and appropriate way that men and women should come together. I said, men and women. Not men and men nor women and women.

Let's move to I Corinthians, the sixth chapter and let's begin in verse 9. And it says here:

"Do you not know that the unrighteous will not inherit the kingdom of God? Do not be deceived. Neither fornicators, nor idolaters, nor adulterers, nor homosexuals, nor sodomites, nor thieves, nor covetous, nor drunkards, nor revilers, nor extortioners will inherit the kingdom of God. And such were some of you. But you were washed, but you were sanctified, but you were justified in the name of the Lord Jesus and by the Spirit of our God."

Just want to make clear that there are specific things that if they are part of your behavior in many contexts, but here we focus on the sexual context, you will not be a part of God's heavenly structure, kingdom, government as it is outline in Revelation the twenty-first chapter.

Now, let's move to Romans the first chapter, because I just want to make a point here. In verse 21, and we're breaking into a thought relative to behavior. It says here:

"Because, although they knew God, they did not glorify Him as God, nor were thankful, but became futile in their thoughts, and their foolish hearts were darkened."

I'm in the first chapter of Romans beginning there in verse 21 and I'm reading from the New King James Version. It says:

"Professing to be wise, they became fools, and changed the glory of the incorruptible God into an image made like corruptible man—and birds and four-footed animals and creeping things. Therefore God also gave them up to uncleanness, in the lusts of their hearts, to dishonor their bodies among themselves,"

God calls certain behavior a dishonoring of your body. Verse 25:

"...who exchanged the truth of God for the lie, and worshiped and served the creature [or, creation] *rather than the Creator, who is blessed forever. Amen. For this reason God gave them up to vile passions. For even their women exchanged the natural use for what is against nature. Likewise also the men, leaving the natural use of the woman, burned in their lust for one another, men with men committing what is shameful, and receiving in themselves the penalty of their error which was due."*

So I just wanted to make it clear. This is not my opinion. And for those of you who operate in the Christian context who accept, support, promote, promulgate, allow, encourage, and/or participate in this behavior, you are contrary to the Word of God. And I'm talking about God, Elohiym. I'm not speaking of any other "god". That's the only God I promulgate. That's the only God I am subject to. And that's the only God whose ideologies, theories, theologies, hypotheses, whatever you want to label it, that I promote. I call it truth. But there's many who will call it something else. That's where I stand.

So there won't be any misunderstanding about any level of context regarding where I am coming from, let's turn to Revelation, the twenty-first chapter, again. And let's go to verse 8. Well I say again, I referenced it earlier, so let's turn to it now. Revelation 21, verse 8. And I am bold because it says here, in verse 8:

"But the cowardly, unbelieving, abominable, murderers, sexually immoral, sorcerers, idolaters, and all liars shall have their part in the lake which burns with fire and brimstone, which is the second death."

So you can see that sexual context is important, because it could put you, if you are a Christian, in jeopardy of the second death, and, if you are a non-Christian, in jeopardy of the second death. See the interesting thing about God is, it does not matter what label you carry, you still come under the rule and dictate of Elohiym, which is a composite of the Father, the Son, and the Holy Spirit. Amen. Do your research and you'll discover that God, Elohiym, is the Originator and everything else is perpetration or perpetrators.

Let's turn to Galatians, the fifth chapter. We also just want to reinforce what the Word of God is saying because sexual context has become a hotbed of controversy. Ministers, pastors, priests, bishops, apostles, prophets, are "tippy toeing" around this issue looking for political correctness.

Galatians, the fifth chapter, let's begin in verse 16. It says here:

"I say then: Walk in the Spirit, and you shall not fulfill the lust of the flesh. For the flesh lusts against the Spirit, and the Spirit against the flesh; and these are contrary to one another, so that you do not do the things that you wish. But if you are led by the Spirit, you are not under the law. Now the works of the flesh are evident, which are: adultery, fornication, uncleanness, lewdness, idolatry, sorcery, hatred, contentions, jealousies, outbursts

of wrath, selfish ambitions, dissensions, heresies, envy, murders, drunkenness, revelries, and the like; of which I tell you beforehand, just as I also told you in time past, that those who practice such things will not inherit the kingdom of God. Let me say this to you again,"*...will not inherit the kingdom of God."*

So don't let Satan come along and say, "thou shill," or "shall inherit the kingdom of God," like he went to Eve and just switched it and twisted it. It's real clear here. So no degree of man's edict, law, or whatever he wants to pass, making same-sex marriages constitutionally correct. You cannot abort the Word of God through any degree of legislation. And America, the United States in particular, among the Americas, is going to suffer for the example that they are setting for the world.

Biblical Reference to Drug Use (46:07 T-6)

And I just want to make a brief point here about the word <u>sorcery</u>. When you look that word up in the Greek, the word is *pharmakeia* or *pharmakeus* and it means "pharmacy" or "drugs." So it's real clear there that if you are engaging in any kind of drug activity, and I am not talking about people who are on medication -- you have to be careful there, also. But I am speaking specifically of those who use drugs to enhance whatever it is they feel they need to enhance.

Amen. So as we deal with that, we need to understand that God is a God of order and direction and instruction. And He knows how to best direct His creation.

Let's turn to Hebrews, the 13th chapter, the 4th verse. It says there: *"Marriage is honorable among all, and the bed undefiled; but fornicators and adulterers God will judge."* Again, relative to sexual context, it has to be in marriage between a man and woman. We've established that with some of the other areas of Scripture that we've talked about.

Weapons of Our Warfare Section Two

Spiritual STDs (47:39 T-7)

Now we need to understand that we are spiritual creations that are housed in physical temples. Let's turn to I Corinthian 6. Because Paul makes an interesting comment that I believe has been misunderstood by too many, not everybody, but too many. Let's begin in verse 12. It says there:

> *"All things are lawful for me, but all things are not helpful. All things are lawful for me, but I will not be brought under the power of any. Foods for the stomach and the stomach for foods, but God will destroy both it and them. Now the body is not for sexual immorality but for the Lord, and the Lord for the body."*

Verse 14 says: *"And God both raised up the Lord and will also raise us up by His power. Do you not know that your bodies are members of Christ?"*

Listen now:

> *..."your bodies are members of Christ? Shall I then take the members of Christ and make them members of a harlot? Certainly not! Or do you not know that he who is joined to a harlot is one body with her? For "the two," He says, "shall become one flesh." But he who is joined to the Lord is one spirit with Him. Flee sexual immorality. Every sin that a man does is outside the body, "* Hear that:*" ...outside the body, but he who commits sexual immorality sins against his own body."* Verse 19: *"Or do you not know that your body is the temple of the Holy Spirit who is in you, whom you have from God, and you are not your own? For you were bought at a price; therefore glorify God in your body and in your spirit, which are God's."*

What Paul is dealing with here is something that I call the spiritual STDs. As you can receive a spiritually transmitted or a sexually transmitted disease, rather, from being with multiple partners you have slept, actually, with every one they've slept with.

You've seen these commercials where they've shown people in the bed. And on one side of the bed, everybody that the woman has slept with and on the other side, everybody the man has slept with. Well, the same is true in our spirit. When we come together outside of the context of God then we are inside of the context of Satan. And we expose ourselves not only to physical contaminants but spiritual contaminants, also. I have counseled individuals, who have tendencies that were never part of their particular behavior, but they came as a result of sleeping around and those individuals who were in a certain mindset transferred through demonic influence that tendency to them. So there can be spiritually transmitted demons, the spiritual STDs.

Now that may be difficult for you to wrap your mind around. But I suggest that you read I Corinthians 6. And why don't we just turn to I Corinthians 3. Because even then Paul had alluded to, or should I say, more than alluded to, the same contextual material. Beginning in verse 16, it says:

> ***"Do you not know that you are the temple of God and that the Spirit of God dwells in you? If anyone defiles the temple of God, God will destroy him. For the temple of God is holy, which temple you are."***

So we're just not giving opinion here. Look at the context in the Word of God. And ask God to give you direction relative to what it is that you need to understand from the material that you're hearing in order to make the proper alignments in your life. So one of the solutions is looking at the Word of God and listening to what God says relative to how you should be conducting yourselves, sexually. And that will eliminate all of the speculatorial political correctness of a man's opinion when you are looking at the Word of God.

Romans, the 5th chapter. And we want to begin there in verse 14. I said earlier in this lecture about the context of Adam and Christ. Here it says:

> ***"Nevertheless death reigned from Adam to Moses, even over those who had not sinned according to the***

likeness of the transgression of Adam, who is a type of Him who was to come." Verse 15: *"**But the free gift is not like the offense. For if by the one man's offense many died, much more the grace of God and the gift by the grace of the one Man, Jesus Christ, abounded to many.**"*

And my point for reading that scripture is, is that Adam and Christ are types. Adam failed but Christ did not. And we need to understand that. Because if Adam would have done what he was supposed to do, then it would not have been necessary for Christ to come and do it in the flesh. So He's succeeded where Adam did not. So we need to understand that. You can also look in I Corinthians 15:45. But, I think that point has been established. And you can look in the context of those Scriptures and realize that what has been stated is accurate.

Adam, Christ, Eve and the Church – The Relationship (55:07 T-8)

The other thing that we need to recognize is that Eve and the Church have a similar relationship to Adam and Christ. Now, in the book of Revelation you can see that God references the Church and uses the imagery of a woman in Revelation 12. Actually in Revelation 12, beginning in verse 1 and ending in verse 17. You can see the whole process of the Church, giving birth, Satan attacking the Church. And again God uses the imagery of a woman to represent the Church. What I would like to do is move to Ephesians the 5th chapter. Because I think this particular relationship of Adam, Christ, Eve, and the Church is explicit and clarified.

Let's look at verse 22 of Ephesians, the 5th chapter. It says here:

"Wives, submit to your own husbands, as to the Lord. For the husband is head of the wife, as also Christ is head of the church; and He is the Savior of the body. Therefore, just as the church is subject to Christ, so let the wives be to their own husbands in everything. Husbands,

love your wives, just as Christ also loved the church and gave Himself for her, that He might sanctify and cleanse her with the washing of water by the word, that He might present her to Himself a glorious church, not having spot or wrinkle or any such thing, but that she should be holy and without blemish."

Verse 28:

"So husbands ought to love their own wives as their own bodies; he who loves his wife loves himself. For no one ever hated his own flesh, but nourishes and cherishes it, just as the Lord does the church. For we are members of His body, of His flesh and of His bones. "For this reason a man shall leave his father and mother and be joined to his wife, and the two shall become one flesh." This is a great mystery, but I speak concerning Christ and the church. Nevertheless let each one of you in particular so love his own wife as himself, and let the wife see that she respects her husband."

Now in reading all of that and looking at that in context, you see the relationship that Christ has with the Church is the same relationship that a man should have with his wife. Christ, who is representative of what Adam should have done in the Garden by protecting his wife from Satan is doing that now by protecting the Church from Satan when the Church is obedient. So there is a tie.

There is a relationship. There is a linkage that is more than just physical, but a highly spiritual relationship that cannot be ignored. It is something that we must be aware of. And something that we must be sensitive to.

Let's turn to Romans the 5th chapter, because it is important again to look at some dialog relative to what we've just stated. And if we begin in verse 6 of Romans the 5th chapter, we see:

"For when we were still without strength, in due time Christ died for the ungodly. For scarcely for a righteous man will one die; yet perhaps for a good man someone would even dare to die. But God demonstrates His own love toward us, in that while we were still sinners, Christ died for us... For if when we were enemies we were reconciled to God through the death of His Son, much more, having been reconciled, we shall be saved by His life. And not only that, but we also rejoice in God through our Lord Jesus Christ, through whom we have now received the reconciliation."

My point is, is that God was committed to us and if you go on and read in Romans 12 –17, as we read earlier, we can see the whole dialog about sin and death coming through one man and then life through another, which is Christ. That the power of God rests in the fact that we need to be moving in His directive and in the context of what He has given us to live relative to marriage and everything else in order to be able to stand against Satan, the evil one, whose primary purpose is to destroy us. And we need to be functioning with the same mind that Christ functioned with when He was on this earth, prior to Him coming to this earth, and as He is functioning now at the right hand of God, as our Mediator, Intercessor, Savior.

We need to understand how important that is. Let's turn to Philippians. Because we need to understand, scripturally, that we have a directive to operate in the mind of Christ. That's again, Philippians, the 2nd chapter, verse 5. It says: *"Let this mind be in you which was also in Christ Jesus."*

A very direct statement. I Corinthians 2:16. I Corinthians 2 and verse 16. Hopefully if you don't have your Bibles with you, you're writing this information down. It says here: *"For who has known the mind of the LORD that he may instruct Him?"* But it says here: *"But we have the mind of Christ."*

Weapons of Our Warfare Section Two

The Mind of Christ (62:55 T-9)

And Paul was saying, you know, if you are a Christian you should be operating in the mind of Christ. Now, in the mind of Christ, can we get a glimpse of what occurs? Let's turn to Luke the 4th chapter. Because now we are going to be moving into more specifically the weapons of our warfare. Because the mind of Christ was set to do a certain category of activities, works, whatever you want to call them, whatever you're comfortable with calling them. But let's look at the 16th verse. It says here in Luke the 4th chapter.

Christ's Mission (6 :55)

"So He came to Nazareth, where He had been brought up. And as His custom was, He went into the synagogue on the Sabbath day, and stood up to read. " Verse 17: *And He was handed the book of the prophet Isaiah. And when He had opened the book, He found the place where it was written: " The Spirit of the LORD is upon Me, Because He has anointed Me preach the gospel to the poor; has sent Me to heal the brokenhearted, proclaim liberty to the captives And recovery of sight to the blind, To set at liberty those who are oppressed; To proclaim the acceptable year of the LORD."*

That was the mind of Christ. That is what was on His mind. That is what the Spirit that was upon Him directed Him to say. And as you read about His acts, His activities, you not only realize that it was a statement, a mission or a purpose statement, but it was the way He conducted His life. So if we're to have the mind of Christ, then these levels of productivity in the way of fruit should be manifested, beginning in our own lives. So, if you were to sum up basically what Christ said His ministry was, it's basically to deliver mankind from Satan's deception, mankind from Satan's deception.

And in that context, there are many ministries, many approaches, many directives, and many aspects, as it says in I

Corinthians 12 that are appropriate under the mantle of God to do. But we want again to focus on direct satanic attack. Let's turn to II Corinthians.

The Weapons of Our Warfare (66:27)

That's II Corinthians, the 10th chapter. And we have cited this text, earlier in the lecture. But I think it is important that we go back to it at this time to maintain our focus relative to what we are dealing with as Christians. As we focus on verse 3, it says:

> *"For though we walk in the flesh, we do not war according to the flesh. For the weapons of our warfare are not carnal but mighty in God for pulling down strongholds, casting down arguments and every high thing that exalts itself against the knowledge of God, bringing every thought into captivity to the obedience of Christ."*

So we are in a struggle to make whatever we are thinking fall under the directive of God, based on the instructions in His Word. Because when we don't do that; we are subject to the strongman and subject to the strongman's directives. Let's turn to Matthew the 12th chapter, because Christ had a few things to say about that, that I think we should note in our discussion. When we move to the 22nd verse of Matthew the 12th chapter:

> *"Then one was brought to Him who was demon-possessed, blind and mute; and He healed him, so that the blind and mute man both spoke and saw. And all the multitudes were amazed and said, "Could this be the Son of David?" Now when the Pharisees heard it they said, "This fellow does not cast out demons except by Beelzebub, the ruler of the demons."*

In other words, it is saying that you cannot do this unless you are working with Satan, which is blasphemous.

> *"But Jesus knew their thoughts, and said to them: "Every kingdom divided against itself is brought to desolation, and every city or house divided against itself will not stand. If Satan casts out Satan, he is divided against himself. How then will his kingdom stand? And if I cast out demons by Beelzebub, by whom do your sons cast them out? Therefore they shall be your judges. But if I cast out demons by the Spirit of God, surely the kingdom of God has come upon you."*

Subduing the Strongman (69:40)

He says here in verse 29:

> *"Or how can one enter a strong man's house and plunder his goods, unless he first binds the strong man? And then he will plunder his house. He who is not with Me is against Me, and he who does not gather with Me scatters abroad."*

And all Christ was pointing out here is that in what He did in freeing this man, He simply went in, subdued the strongman who was Satan, or Satan's representative, and freed this human being as He stated His mission was in Luke the 4th chapter. So we need to realize that there is a battle. Many religious individuals won't understand it, in the proper context, as the Pharisees and Sadducees did not understand it, when Christ engaged in it.

But let's move to chapter 11 of Luke because there are some other dialog we need to take a look at. When we focus on verse 14, and it says here:

> *"And He was casting out a demon, and it was mute. So it was, when the demon had gone out, that the mute spoke; and the multitudes marveled. But some of them*

said, "He casts out demons by Beelzebub, the ruler of the demons." Others, testing Him, sought from Him a sign from heaven. But He, knowing their thoughts, said to them: "Every kingdom divided against itself is brought to desolation, and a house divided against a house falls."

And in verse 18 it says:

"If Satan also is divided against himself, how will his kingdom stand? Because you say I cast out demons by Beelzebub. And if I cast out demons by Beelzebub, by whom do your sons cast them out?"

And again we can see this is a recount of what we read in Matthew, but just to show you that it was a notable event that Matthew and Luke pointed it out. But I want to focus on verse, well beginning in verse 24. It says:

Staying Free (72:14 T-10)

"When an unclean spirit goes out of a man, he goes through dry places, seeking rest; and finding none, he says, 'I will return to my house from which I came.' And when he comes, he finds it swept and put in order. Then he goes and takes with him seven other spirits more wicked than himself, and they enter and dwell there; and the last state of that man is worse than the first."

First of all, when it talks about "put in order" it means that he may be in order of living his life the same way he was prior to him being delivered, therefore making himself more vulnerable to attack. What Christ was trying to point out here is that when you engage in the activity of delivering people or if you engage in activity of making changes in your life, when you go back to doing those things (sin), when you order your life in such a way that the enemy can come back in with the same attitudes, he's going to bring in seven other attitudes, or motivations, or sins, or levels of evil. And your struggle is going to be compounded because you walked back into a scenario, making a conscious decision to do so. And you didn't fill those vacant vacuumed areas with the Word of God. So my point is this: Once we have been delivered from a stronghold, in order to keep that stronghold from regaining its grip and bringing other areas of strongholds to maintain that grip, we must walk in the degree of deliverance which we have received. And it is important that we understand that, because our deliverance is predicated on that process. And we do have access to the power to be able to confront those things and defeat them the way Christ demonstrated and modeled for us.

So as we move into the next segment, we're going to be discussing the actual weapons and how we can use them relative to our deliverance in this warfare. May God bless you for listening to CD #2. Continue on and be blessed by completing the whole series, by listening to CD #3. God bless you!

Weapons of Our Warfare Section Two

Weapons of Our Warfare Section Three

Weapons of Our Warfare Section Three

Table of Contents

Lecture Section Three..57
    Introduction T-1..62
        We Have been Given
        Authority 62
    John 16:5 T-2..63
        The Power to Operate....................64
        Importance of Fasting
        and Prayer 64
    Activities in Healing and Deliverance T-3 65
        Book Referrals..................................66
        Strongman's His Name,
        What's His Game? 66
        Breaking Strongholds in the African
        American Family 67
        Prayer of Deliverance
        by Derek Prince...............................68
    Spirit of Divination T-4 69
        Deuteronomy 18:9-13 69
        Familiar Spirit.................................70
    Who We Are at War T-5...................................71
        II Corinthians 10:3-4 71
        Leviticus 20:27 72
    Spirit of Jealousy T-6.......................................72

Weapons of Our Warfare Section Three

Table of Contents

Numbers 5:14 73
The Lying Spirit 73
Revelation 21:8 74
Perverse Spirit 75
Spirit of Haughtiness 75
Job 41:34 76
Spirit of Heaviness 77
Spirit of Whoredom T-7 77
Spirit of Infirmity 78
Dumb and Deaf Spirit 79
Spirit of Bondage 80
Spirit of Fear T-8 82
Seducing Spirit................................83
Spirit of Antichrist T-9 84
Spirit of Error 85
Spirit of Death T-10 86

Weapons of Our Warfare Section Three

Introduction (T-1)

Hello again, this is Dr. Ernest Maddox and if you have been listening to this series called Weapons of Our Warfare, you know we are at the point now where we are going to go into the weapons, the weaponry, and what we have been given by God in the Scripture, relative to authority, to be able to wage this war.

We Have Been Given Authority (0:34)

We have been given authority over all the power of the enemy that includes Satan, Beelzebub, and every demon, illness, etc. Let's turn to Luke the 10th chapter, verse 17. It says, Then the seventy returned with joy, saying, *"Lord, even the demons are subject to us in Your name. And He said to them,"* the "He" being Christ, *"I saw Satan fall like lightning from heaven. Behold, I give you the authority to trample on serpents and scorpions, and over all the power of the enemy, and nothing shall by any means hurt you."*

And you know by reading Revelation 12 and in other places that the serpent refers to Satan. Verse 20, it says, *"Nevertheless do not rejoice in this, that the spirits are subject to you"*... Christ says don't get bent out of shape about that, they are subject to you. I've given you that authority, ...but rather rejoice because your names are written in heaven.

See our power comes from God, who is where our authority comes from, that's where our power comes from, that's where our directive comes from, to be able to do what we need to do in this war. Let's turn to Matthew the 18th chapter and look at verse 18. That's Matthew 18:18. It says, *"Assuredly, I say to you, whatever you bind on earth will be bound in heaven, and whatever you loose on earth will be loosed in heaven."*

And it's not talking about the throne of God. It's talking about the heavenly places where principalities dwell. Because we can't bind anything at God's throne. This is talking about spiritual warfare, and it says here,

"Again I say to you that if two of you agree on earth concerning anything that they ask, it will be done for them by My Father in heaven." In other words, the power comes from heaven. For where two or three are gathered together in My name, I am there in the midst of them.(Mat. 18:19-20)

So God says "I'll be there," Christ says, "I'll be there in your midst." I'm there in you and I'm there in the midst. So we have the power to bind and to loose. We have the power to bind the enemy, and to loose the power of the Holy Spirit. Not that we can hold the Holy Spirit in bondage. It simply means that we give our free will over to God, and free ourselves, and make ourselves accessible. What is the scriptural support for that? We all know that the text says we shouldn't grieve the Holy Spirit. We grieve the Holy Spirit by forbidding it to do what God has sent it to do in us.

John 16:5 (3:47 T-2)

Let's turn to John the sixteenth chapter, and I just want to take a moment and go to that text because we need to recognize the power of the Holy Spirit and what the Holy Spirit can and will do in us. In **John 16:5** it says, **"But now I go away to Him who sent Me, and none of you asks Me, 'Where are You going?"** And Christ is talking about His ascension, His pending crucifixion,

"But because I have said these things to you, sorrow has filled your heart. Nevertheless I tell you the truth. It is to your advantage that I go away; for if I do not go away, the Helper will not come to you; but if I depart, I will send Him to you. And when He has come."

The helper is the Holy Spirit.

"He will convict the world of sin, and of righteousness, and of judgment: of sin, because they do not believe in Me; of righteousness, because I go to My Father

and you see Me no more; of judgment, because the ruler of this world is judged. (John 16:8-11)

The Power to Operate (4:55)

And I just want to reinforce what I said earlier about the power of God and the Holy Spirit and us grieving it, because we, with our behavior, can resist what God is doing, therefore, allowing the enemy to have inroads that he should not have, being weak in what we should be doing with the Holy Spirit that we have received from God in order to do the things that He has directed us to do. Let's turn to II Timothy 1:7, because we have the power to operate. It says, *"For God has not given us a spirit of fear, but of power and of love and of a sound mind."*

Importance of Fasting and Prayer (5:47)

We have power to take proactive action, the love to administer the balance, and the sound mindedness not to be confused about who's doing the work, God. Healing and deliverance go hand-in-hand with prayer and fasting. There are things that we must do in order to be able to operate in the power of God at a maximum level or operating with the mind of Christ, as we have earlier established. Let's turn to Matthew the 17th chapter and look at a grouping of verses here that I think will shed some light on the statement of being able to move in the power of God, using the elements of fasting and prayer.

Matthew 17:14 and it states, "And when they had come to the multitude, a man came to Him, kneeling down to Him and saying, Lord, have mercy on my son, for he is an epileptic and suffers severely; for he often falls into the fire and often into the water. So I brought him to Your disciples, but they could not cure him. Then Jesus answered and said, O faithless and perverse generation, how long shall I be with you? How long shall I bear with you? Bring him here to Me."

Christ was expressing concerns about, number one, His disciples, but the world in general, not being able to function in the power. And Jesus rebuked the demon, and it came out of him. Now here you have a combination of a disease connected with demonic influence, and Jesus rebuked the demon and it came out, and the child was cured. Healing and deliverance go hand in hand,...from that very hour.

> *"Matthew 17:19, Then the disciples came to Jesus privately and said, "Why could we not cast it out?" So Jesus said to them, "Because of your unbelief; for assuredly, I say to you, if you have faith as a mustard seed, you will say to this mountain, 'Move from here to there,' and it will move; and nothing will be impossible for you.*

In verse 21 He says, *"However, this kind does not go out except by prayer and fasting."* "This kind," He talks about that kind of demon, epileptic demon, has to be encountered through a life of prayer and fasting, (he was also referring to unbelief). So we need, we need to, as warring Christians, to be in a state of prayer and fasting, and making prayer a daily activity along with Bible study and fasting a regular activity. Not just once every year or once every five (5) years, and fasting is just not missing breakfast that year.

In the Old Testament, the Day of Atonement fast was considered 24 hours without anything. There are other forms of fasting. There are books that have been written on them, I won't go into that now. But in order to move in the level and at the level of power that you need to be able to move in, you need to be in a state of fasting and prayer coupled with regular daily Bible study, knowing what the Word of God says.

Activities in Healing and Deliverance (9:54 T-3)

Now, when we talk about intervention, healing and deliverance and praying, there are several activities that occur. You know, some people lay on hands, some individuals speak in tongues, some have a word of knowledge. All of these are established in the Word.

For example:

Laying on of hands can be found in Matthew 8:14-15, Mark 16:18, Luke 4:40-41, Luke 13:10-13. Fallen in the Spirit can be found in several places: Deuteronomy 9:18, John 18:4-6, Acts 9:3-6. The word of knowledge can be found in I Corinthians 12, look at verses 1 and 8, and John 4:29. Speaking in tongues: I Corinthians12:1 and 10, also I Corinthians 14 the whole chapter deals with speaking in tongues, Acts 2:1-4.

So these are activities that could occur doing intervention or deliverance prayer, they are not necessary, and they are not indicative of somebody being super-spiritual. We want to recognize that it's not the gifts that Christ says we should be known, but by our fruit.

Book Referrals
Strongman's His Name, What's His Game? (11:50)

At this point, I want to draw your attention to a book entitled "Strongman's His Name, What's His Game?" by Drs. Jerry and Carol Robeson. It describes 16 strongmen, or spirits, that attack human beings. The Spirit of Divination, Familiar Spirit, Spirit of Jealousy, Lying Spirit, Perverse Spirit, Spirit of Haughtiness, which is Pride, Spirit of Heaviness, Spirit of Whoredoms, Spirit of Infirmity, Dumb and Deaf Spirit, Spirit of Bondage, Spirit of Fear, Seducing Spirits, Spirit of Antichrist, Spirit of Error, and Spirit of Death. Now these spirits can operate in combinations, isolation, strongmen will use sub-spirits. I would recommend that you get the book. It's a very easy book to read. Great introductory book relative to the arena of spiritual warfare.

Weapons of Our Warfare Section Three

__Breaking Strongholds in the African American Family (13:01)__

There's also another book that I want to point out, that deals with Breaking Strongholds in the African-American Family and that is the title of the book by Dr. Clarence Walker, and he breaks it down into three categories: Males, females and youth. Fear of intimacy syndrome. This is under the male: bloody warrior syndrome, pride syndrome, polygamy sexuality syndrome.

Under the female is the Jezebel syndrome, the cutting tongue, co-dependency, the Tamar complex, and you should read about the Tamar complex because it's one of David's daughters who is sexually molested by one of her brothers, and it creates a whole scenario, but you should read the story.

Under the "Youth," Clarence Walker, Dr. Walker talks about: tribalism syndrome, out of wedlock deadlock, negative music and low self-esteem.

Now these are just basic areas and just two books that I would recommend. And I would recommend Clarence Walker's book for any group of people, not just African-Americans, as I would recommend the Robeson book for any group of people. So these are books that I would encourage the beginner or the novice, relative to spiritual warfare, to read. They are good beginning foundational books. And I'm not saying that I agree with everything that's said in these books. I'm simply saying that these are good foundational beginning points to give a broader understanding of spiritual warfare and what that entails; and how we can approach some of the things that are occurring in our lives, relative to what we are facing in the way of challenges and unshakable behaviors and impulses. I'm telling you now that these things that seem to have a life of their own, actually do have a life of their own, and that life is demonic and it is influencing you and having an impact on your life.

Prayer of Deliverance by Derek Prince (15:37)

So what I would like to do now is share a prayer of deliverance from Derek Prince's ministry (via "Pigs In The Parlor"). I'm just going to read that prayer, and hopefully you will listen, maybe you will participate, that is your decision. It begins:

"Lord Jesus Christ, I believe you died on the cross for my sins and rose again from the dead, you redeemed me by your blood and I belong to you and I want to live for you.

I confess all my sins, known and unknown. I'm sorry for them all, I renounce them all, I forgive all others as I want you to forgive me. Forgive me now and cleanse me with your blood. I thank you for the blood of Jesus Christ which cleanses me now from all sin and I come to you now as my deliverer. You know my special needs, the thing that binds and torments, that defiles, that evil spirit, that unclean spirit, I claim the promise of your word, Whosoever that calls on the name of the Lord shall be delivered. I call upon you now, in the name of the Lord Jesus Christ, deliver me and set me free. Satan, I renounce you and all your works. I loose myself from you in the name of Jesus and I command you to leave me right now, in Jesus' name, Amen." (Hammond, 1973, p.107)

Now this is just a basic simple prayer of deliverance, you can agree or not agree. You can choose your own wording, or for those who may not have had a clue or an idea of how to approach deliverance prayer, I shared this with you, and for you.

Now what I would like to do is go back at this point and look at very specifically some of the things that we talked about, in the way of spirits, and maybe go into a little more detail about how some of them operate in your life and in my life. And I'm actually going to use the book by Robeson and Robeson to briefly go over some of the elements contained in the description of how some of these demonic spirits operate in the lives of human beings to destroy them.

Spirit of Divination (18:50 T-4)

Now first of all the "spirit of divination." The dictionary defines that as the practice of attempting to foretell the future events or discover hidden knowledge by occult or supernatural means. This simply means that you should not be dealing with horoscopes, fortunetelling, palm reading, crystal ballism, tarot cards. You should not be engaged in any of those activities. Because when you do engage in them, you are exposing yourself to witchcraft, necromancy, warlockism which is nothing but a male witch, sorcery. You are not to engage in those activities, because you will create serious spiritual problems for yourself, and for those who are in your family.

Now those who are engaged in drug use will discover that you are already tied up in divination, because in sorcery and in witchcraft and satanism, drugs are used to establish links with the demonic realm. So if you are engaging in those activities, you are already in need of deliverance. You are already in need of help. And you need to ask God for direction. You need to get down on your knees, right now in fact, and ask God for His help and direction regarding this. Because if you do not, then you are headed for destruction and loss of life. But before you actually lose your life, you're going to lose quality of life. As it says in John and I'll reference that later, but now I want to go to Deuteronomy the 18th chapter, beginning in verse 9. And it says:

Deuteronomy 18:9–13 (21:13)

"When you come into the land which the LORD your God is giving you, you shall not learn to follow the abominations of those nations. There shall not be found among you anyone who makes his son or his daughter pass through the fire, or one who practices witchcraft, or a soothsayer, or one who interprets omens, or a sorcerer, or one who conjures spells, or a medium, or a spiritist, or one who calls up the dead. For all who do these things are an abomination to the LORD and because of these

abominations the LORD your God drives them out from before you. You shall be blameless before the LORD your God."

And you can see here where God has a serious problem with that whole process. Now there are other scriptures that we could go to, but I think that establishes the foundation, and makes it clear that biblically, the things that some of us, especially some of us Christians, we do as a matter of daily habit and take for granted. I know Christians who go get their palms read. I know Christians who have spiritualists as their guides and won't listen to their pastors, but will listen to the spiritualists.

Familiar Spirit (22:59)

But let's move to the next spirit that is listed in the Robeson book: familiar spirit. Now a familiar spirit and a spirit of divination are very similar in nature; in fact, they can usually be under one strongman or in a gang under one strongman. But a familiar spirit is usually involved in the areas of necromancy, consulting with the dead, mediums, clairvoyance, yoga, psychic powers and prophecy that is not from God, transcendental meditation, extra-sensory perception, involved in the areas that conjure up information.

The ability to contact the spirits is often passed from one generation to the next within receptive families, which may account, in part, for its name. So these demonic spirits operate within the context of being passed on from one family member to another, engaging in activities that are anti-God by their description and performing activities outside of the guidelines of the Holy Spirit, which are contained in the Word of God, between the first chapter, or the first verse, should I say, of Genesis to the last verse of Revelation.

And this spirit deals with and operates in a category of control and family bondage. It's just that basic. And I think that we have already dealt with the scriptural basis for that in the chapter we just read. So you need to understand that there are elements there that we need to be able to confront with the Word of God and the power of God.

Who We Are at War With
Ephesians 6:10-12 (25:24 T-5)

Let's turn to Ephesians just as a refresher, or a memory prompter, relative to who we are sincerely at war with. That's Ephesians the 6th chapter, verse 10:

> *"Finally, my brethren, be strong in the Lord and in the power of His might. Put on the whole armor of God that you may be able to stand against the wiles of the devil. For we do not wrestle against flesh and blood, but against principalities, against powers, against the rulers of the darkness of this age, against spiritual hosts of wickedness in the heavenly places."*

So our battle is with spiritual wickedness in high places.

II Corinthians 10:3-4 (26:18)

Let's turn to II Corinthians the tenth chapter, because again we've used these scriptures before, but now we want to use them in the light of this current level of discussion. Verse 3, II Corinthians the 10th chapter,

> '*For though we walk in the flesh, we do not war according to the flesh. For the weapons of our warfare are not carnal but mighty in God for pulling down strongholds,...*"

That is what we are about as Christians, breaking the strong grips in our lives, destroying the strongholds. The enemy has many weapons in his arsenal, but we have been given authority and power over all of them. The spirit of divination and the familiar spirit are just two.

Leviticus 20:27 (27:18)

Now before we move on to the next spirit or the next strongman, let's please turn to Leviticus 20, the 27th verse. That's Leviticus the 20th chapter, and we're going to land at verse 27. It says here: *"A man or a woman who is a medium, or who has familiar spirits, shall surely be put to death; they shall stone them with stones. Their blood shall be upon them. "*

I just wanted to add that relative to familiar spirits. You know we talked about that just before we moved into the statement that I just made. We talked about the familiar spirit and we also talked about the spirit of divination. So I just wanted to close that particular conversation out relative to the spirit or familiar spirits, with that scripture.

Spirit of Jealousy (28:22 T-6)

Now we want to move on to the spirit of jealousy. The spirit of jealousy has many aspects to it. Murder, revenge, anger, rage, cruelty, extreme competition, strife, hatred, contention, envy, and it also causes division. The spirit of jealousy is what led Cain to kill Abel. And it is a very powerful spirit. In James the 3rd chapter, and we won't turn there; if you read somewhere around verses 13, 14, 15 and 16, it talks about where there is envy, and I'm paraphrasing now, and strife there is every evil work. So it is basically saying that where you have a spirit of jealousy that breeds these things, you open the door to all types of demonic activity. Because Satan was jealous, he attempted to take over the throne of God.

Ezekiel 28, verses 12 through 19 and Isaiah 14, verses 12 through 14, you can see where that is articulated. But now let's turn to Numbers the fifth chapter, and we want to stop there in verse 14. That's Numbers the 5th chapter and we want to look at verse 14; and as I'm finding it also, amen, we land here in verse 14. It says:

Weapons of Our Warfare Section Three

Numbers 5:14–15 (30:02)

"If the spirit of jealousy comes upon him and he becomes jealous of his wife, who has defiled herself; or if the spirit of jealousy comes upon him and he becomes jealous of his wife, although she has not defiled herself-- then the man shall bring his wife to the priest. He shall bring the offering required for her."

And it's going into what should happen if there is an issue of jealousy. But there is a spirit of jealousy, and that's my point. Here in verse 14 of Numbers the 5th chapter that the spirit of jealousy does exist. And that is something we need to be aware of, we need to be concerned about. Jealousy, along with pride, are probably the oldest sins in the universe, and this is a combination of what Satan had when he attempted to dethrone God our Father- - Elohiym, the Ruler and Creator and Designer and Originator of the whole universe. So that's something that I wanted to share regarding the spirit of jealousy.

The Lying Spirit (31:22)

Now let's move on to the lying spirit. There is a lying spirit and we can simply just go to John the 8th chapter. There are many places we could go for that, but let's go to John the 8th chapter, because Christ makes a very dogmatic and unapologetic statement regarding the lying spirit and its origin. *John 8:44*, that's the Gospel of John. It says,

"You are of your father the devil, and the desires of your father you want to do. He was a murderer from the beginning, and does not stand in the truth, because there is no truth in him. When he speaks a lie, he speaks from his own resources, for he is a liar and the father of it."

Very clear, Satan is the father of lies, and Satan is a spirit, a very perverse, demonic spirit. So therefore it's another aspect of the spiritual realm and the battle that we are engaged in. We have to be careful that we are not engaged in that kind of activity. And I just want to spend a few more moments on this particular spirit. I think that it's important that you understand how God feels about this. Turn to Proverbs the 6th chapter, verse 16. That's Proverbs the 6th chapter, verse 16 and it starts here saying, ***"These six things the LORD hates, Yes, seven are an abomination to Him: A proud look, A lying tongue."*** And it has two of the spirits there, ***"Hands that shed innocent blood, A heart that devises wicked plans, Feet that are swift in running to evil, A false witness who speaks lies."*** So He names it twice - - a lying tongue and a false witness who speaks lies, ***"and one who sows discord among brethren."***

Usually a liar is one who sows discord among brethren. So you can see that God has an attitude, not just with liars, but with all perverse strongmen spirits. But He has a particular articulated dislike for the lying spirit.

Revelation 21:8 (34:13)

Now let's turn to Revelation 21 and let's focus in on verse 8, because again there is an interesting statement here regarding liars, lying and that whole mentality that emanates from Satan himself.
Verse 8, it says ***"But the cowardly..."***, And we're breaking into a context here that talks about the return of the Father to this earth, bringing New Jerusalem, but that's another topic. I just want to focus on verse 8, but also acknowledge that we are breaking into a thought and a concept here. And it says:

> ***"But the cowardly, unbelieving, abominable, murderers, sexually immoral, sorcerers, idolaters, and all liars shall have their part in the lake which burns with fire and brimstone, which is the second death."***

So again, as God describes the mentalities and the attitudes and the spirits and the strongmen who promulgate these spirits and inflict, affect and infect us with these attitudes, if we allow this to happen, we will end up victims of the second death, and liars are included in that. So, I just wanted to make that clear and just spend a couple of more moments on the lying spirit, probably more so than the others at this time.

Perverse Spirit (35:54)

Now, the next spirit we want to address is the perverse spirit. And a perverse spirit is one that… Well let's look at Isaiah 19:14. It says,

> ***"The LORD hath mingled a perverse spirit in the midst thereof: and they have caused Egypt to err in every work thereof, as a drunken [man] staggereth in his vomit. (KJV)"***

So God is saying here that a perverse spirit is one that causes our behavior to be twisted. In Romans 1:28 it states, ***"And even as they did not like to retain God in [their] knowledge, God gave them over to a reprobate mind, to do those things which are not convenient." (KJV)***

A perverse spirit is a twisted, broken spirit. It causes evil actions. You usually have atheists that are operating in that spirit. Abortion is the result of that spirit. Sex perversions, twisting the Word, chronic worrying, contentions, are just a few of the by-products of a perverse spirit. So again here is one of the strongmen who invade our lives as Christians and you don't even have to be a Christian to be invaded by these strongmen. They twist and try to derail us from what God has directed us to do in our lives.

Spirit of Haughtiness (37:44)

Now the next spirit we want to take a look at is the spirit of haughtiness. The spirit of haughtiness. And usually what comes with that is: arrogance, pride, idleness, being scornful, obstinate, self-deception, rebellion, and self-righteousness are just a few of the by-products of this spirit. Now let's turn to Proverbs 16 and we want to focus on verse 18; that's Proverbs 16, verse 18. And there are many areas in the Scriptures that deal with this particular mindset. We don't have time to address them all. It says in verse 18: **"Pride goes before destruction and a haughty spirit before a fall."** Verse 19, and it says here, **"Better to be of a humble spirit with the lowly, Than to divide the spoil with the proud."** So again we see that these spirits, or these strongmen, or these perverse spirits, and they are a part of Satan's arsenal. They're not the only thing that he uses in his arsenal, but they are a big part of his arsenal.

Job 41:34 (39:16)

Let's turn to Job because I want to point out something that may be interesting to some of you. Some of you may be fully aware of it because you've probably studied Job to a great degree. We want to turn to Job, chapter 41 and we want to go to the 34th verse, which is actually the last verse before Job goes into his repentant phase. And it says there, **"He beholds every high thing; He is king over all the children of pride."**

And if you are familiar with chapter 41 at all, it is talking about Leviathan. This is a spiritual entity that is a principality that lords over the spirit of pride, or is the spirit of pride, or controlling spirit of pride, because when you read verse 34, and let's read it again, **"He beholds..."** Talking about Leviathan**..."every high thing; He is king over all the children of pride."**

That is no physical being, be it sea creature, or human being. It is talking about something with the power to control everybody who has pride, and can see and lord over those who have pride. It's a strongman, it's a principality and the name is Leviathan. So I just wanted to point that out because right after that Job went into a state of repentance and acknowledged that he knew that God knew everything that he was thinking, or knew every purpose that was in his heart, and in his heart there was some degree of pride that he needed to repent of. Amen.

Spirit of Heaviness (41:10)

So now we want to go to the spirit of heaviness, and with the spirit of heaviness some of the by-products or should I say, behaviors, that will accompany this particular stronghold/spirit is excessive mourning, sorrow and grief, insomnia, broken-heartedness, despair and dejection, depression, suicidal thoughts, inner hurts and torn spirit, self-pity, people who seem to have weightedness in their lives at all times where they can't seem to be free from worry or concern. That is a spirit, it is not natural to mourn or to grieve two or three years. That is not natural. And when it goes beyond the natural context, and that could vary for different individuals, but we can all sense when it becomes a burden.

In *Isaiah 61:3* it says, *"To appoint unto them that mourn in Zion, to give unto them beauty for ashes, the oil of joy for mourning, the garment of praise for the spirit of heaviness." (KJV)*

So this is what God says about that context. We should have for those who mourn in Zion, we need to give them beauty for ashes, the oil of joy for mourning, and the garment of praise for the spirit of heaviness. So that's scriptural evidence that we should not fall into a state of perpetual heaviness, because it is not of God. It is a demonic spirit.

Spirit of Whoredom (43:12 T-7)

The next spirit that we want to address is the spirit of whoredom. That's unfaithfulness, adultery, prostitution, love of money, chronic dissatisfaction, excessive appetite, fornication (again), idolatry, and worldliness. We have to be very careful because a lot of times we do not whore in our flesh, but in our spirit, and we pursue things that God would not have us pursue. But we pursue them because we want them; we think that they are good for us; we think we should have them, we believe that other people have them and if they are good for them, these things should be good for us. But we fail to recognize that everything that is good for someone else may not be the best thing for us. Alcohol, standing on its own and used in moderation, is not necessarily evil, it's the excessive use of it which creates a problem. So let's look at **Hosea 5:4:** *"They do not direct their deeds toward turning to their God. For the spirit of harlotry is in their midst, and they do not know the Lord."*

So God says that there's a spirit that causes one to act and behave in a way that leads them away from Him, a harlot spirit, or the spirit of whoredom. So that is another point of attack that the enemy uses. Sexual impulses being used out of the proper context, and out of the proper context simply means using them outside of the Word of God.

Spirit of Infirmity (45:30)

Now the next spirit we want to address is the spirit of infirmity, which is an illness, sickness, back trouble, having arthritis, lingering disorders like diabetes, heart trouble that is generated by a spirit. Now it causes physical manifestations. But let's look at Luke the 13th chapter, because there's a great controversy that has developed around people seeking professional, so-called professional medical advice and relying on God. There has to be a degree of balance. Luke the 13th chapter and we'll begin here in verse 11. It says,

> *"And behold, there was a woman who had a spirit of infirmity eighteen years, and was bent over and could in no way raise herself up. But when Jesus saw her, He called her to Him and said to her, "Woman, you are loosed from your infirmity." And He laid His hands on her, and immediately she was made straight, and glorified God."*

You could see here that in this particular case the spirit of infirmity caused this woman to have a condition in her back or spine that would not allow her to walk upright and God laid hands on her, in the form of Jesus Christ, healed that condition, and freed her from that. And no doubt the spirit of infirmity caused that, because that is how it's described here.

But that's not the only thing it can create; arthritis and many other things. But these things can be addressed through the power of prayer. Now, am I saying that you should not seek medical advice? No, I am not. I'm saying, that's a decision you should make. Wisdom should be used. You should know what is happening in your body. You should seek the advice of those who have been trained to give you a medical evaluation. But, if you are a Christian, your focus in healing should be on God, and your Lord and Savior, Jesus Christ, because by His stripes you were or are healed. So that is the position relative to that. And there should be a degree of balance.

Dumb and Deaf Spirit (48:19)

Now let's look at the dumb and deaf spirit. Dumb and deaf, deaf mute, crying is connected with that, tearing, ear problems, mental illness, blindness, connected with seizures and epilepsy, pinning away or just allowing yourself to just wane away, gnashing of teeth, foaming at the mouth, are all manifestations of this demonic spirit. Now why don't we just take a look at one incident here, scripturally, relative to that, and that would be in Mark the 9th chapter, Mark 9, and just look at an incident that occurred. That's Mark 9:17, and in the 17th verse it says,

> *"Then one of the crowd answered and said, "Teacher, I brought You my son, who has a mute spirit. And wherever it seizes him, it throws him down; he foams at the mouth, gnashes his teeth, and becomes rigid. So I spoke to Your disciples, that they should cast it out, but they could not."*

Now notice that he says that they should cast it out. Now he's talking about a spirit.

> *"And Christ answered him and said, "O faithless generation, how long shall I be with you? How long shall I bear with you? Bring him to Me." Then they brought him to Him. And when he saw Him, immediately the spirit*

convulsed him, and he fell on the ground and wallowed, foaming at the mouth. So He asked his father, "How long has this been happening to him?" And he said, "From childhood. And often he has thrown him both into the fire and into the water to destroy him. But if You can do anything, have compassion on us and help us." Jesus said to him, "If you can believe, all things are possible to him who believes." Immediately the father of the child cried out and said with tears, "Lord, I believe; help my unbelief!" When Jesus saw that the people came running together, He rebuked the unclean spirit, saying to it, "Deaf and dumb spirit, I command you, come out of him and enter him no more!"

Very clear.

"Then the spirit cried out, convulsed him greatly, and came out of him. And he became as one dead, so that many said, "He is dead." But Jesus took him by the hand and lifted him up, and he arose. And when He had come into the house, His disciples asked Him privately, "Why could we not cast it out?" So He said to them, "This kind can come out by nothing but prayer and fasting."

So there are two messages here. Number 1: These things can be addressed but you have to have a close relationship with God through prayer and fasting. So again, this is another one of Satan's weapons that he uses against human beings.

Spirit of Bondage (52:10)

Now let's look at this spirit of bondage which has under its umbrella, so to speak, fear, addiction (which is drugs), captivity to Satan, (which is cultism), fear of death, a servant of corruption mentality, compulsive sin, which people find themselves unable to stop or to break away from, sin that continuously manifests itself and there seems to be no power to resist; but we do have power.

Again, let me reference Luke the 10th chapter. Now you've heard this if you've been listening to this series of lectures. You've heard this scripture more than once and you'll probably hear it again. Luke 10 starting in verse 17.

It says, *"**Then the seventy returned with joy, saying, "Lord, even the demons are subject to us in Your name.***" And Christ said, and I'm going to read what it says here but we're talking about Christ:

Luke 10:18-19, "And He said to them, "I saw Satan fall like lightning from heaven. Behold, I give you the authority to trample on serpents and scorpions, and over all the power of the enemy, and nothing shall by any means hurt you."

So we do have power over the enemy, including the spirit of bondage. Let's turn to Romans the 8th chapter, verse 15, that's **Romans 8:15**, it says here, *"**For you have not received the spirit of bondage again to fear, you have received the spirit of adoption, whereby we cry Abba Father"…(KJV)***

Which means "Big Daddy." So, in other words, we have not received a spirit of bondage from God. So we don't need to fear that. We have a spirit of adoption. Full <u>Son Hood</u> from God, to do everything that Christ said we should be able to do over the power of the enemy in Luke the 10th chapter beginning around verse 17. So we don't have to be subject to compulsiveness, addictive behavior. We don't have to be servants to corruption. We don't have to submit to manipulation and we don't have to say to ourselves, "I just don't have the strength." None of us has the strength. The strength comes from God. And we need to be thankful for that and embrace that, and use that as a weapon against everything the enemy can throw at us.

Weapons of Our Warfare Section Three

Spirit of Fear (55:16 T-8)

Now let's move to the spirit of fear. And again we can talk about II Timothy 1:7 and I'll just state it again, God has not given us the spirit of fear, phobias, torment, horror, fear of man, nightmares, anxiety. *"God has not given us that spirit, but a spirit of power, love and a sound mind."*

There are a couple of kinds of fear. There are actually two different kinds: positive and negative. Positive fear is a natural sort, a protection that keeps us from hurting ourselves: fear of fire, fear of jumping off a 20-story building. We don't stick our hand in a blazing fire because we know it will do permanent damage to our body. We could characterize this fear more as a deep respect and that's natural.

Then there's a level of fear, a spiritual fear that we should have for our God and our Creator. In Psalms 111:10 it states, *"The fear of the Lord is the beginning of wisdom."* So that's not a trembling fear, that's not a fear that brings trepidation, where you are running and hiding like you are being chased by a lion, but it is a fear that causes us to seek the Word of God to submit to it.

A natural, positive fear can escalate to the point that the spirit of fear takes over. Now here's the difference: A negative fear develops when a positive fear is taken to the extreme. A spirit of fear is at work when our spiritual vitality is affected. Negative fear chokes the elements of faith, joy, peace and love, paralyzes us, can't do what we need to do, like a fear of coming out of the house, that's an unnatural fear. The fear of being in public places; that's an unnatural fear. And when that occurs, a demon, or the demon, or the spirit, or the strongman, of fear has entered into your life. And we need to focus on the spirit and the power of God, have counseling from a solid ministerial base, in order to overcome this enemy.

Seducing Spirit (57:53)

Let's move on now to the seducing spirit, which has many elements to it. Usually it involves being lured into things that are not godly. You know, attractions, deceptions, fascinations, being led or enticed by things that may appear to be interesting and/or nice, not within the godly context of Christianity. Let's turn to I Timothy 4th chapter, 1st verse, and let us begin reading here. It says,

> *"Now the Spirit expressly says that in latter times some will depart from the faith, giving heed to deceiving spirits and doctrines of demons.* Verse 2: *Speaking lies in hypocrisy, having their own conscience seared with a hot iron."*

In other words, these seducing spirits can sear your conscience and make you dull to the impact of what you are doing. That's why we have people now who are having sex with animals, babies, all kind of perverted activity, killing people during sex, paying people to be able to arrange those kind of things, having whole tours around having sex with teenagers in the Orient. And this is documented. This is because of a seducing spirit, or a group of seducing spirits that are attacking mankind in general, and specifically, the Church. And we need to be aware and sensitive to that.

There are many churches that have serious sexual activity vices going on and they don't want to address them. Pastors sleeping with young women, leaders who are playing sexual games with women and men, homosexuality, the whole shot, but we are trying to be so politically correct, we don't want to address it. Well, I'll just simply say to you, you can politically correct yourself right into the second death. When we take a politically correct position against Christ, we take a politically correct position against God, and it does have consequences: eternal death.

Spirit of Antichrist (60:34 T-9)

Now we want to talk about the diabolical spirit of antichrist. The Spirit of Antichrist. You deny the deity of Christ. You deny His existence. You deny His teachings. You deny the fact that He was human as well as God. You deceive and manipulate His Word, and you operate in lawlessness, which is totally separate from where Christ is. Let's turn to I John, I John the 4th chapter and it just simply says here.

> *1 John 4:3, And every spirit that confesseth not that Jesus Christ is come in the flesh is not of God: and this is that [spirit] of antichrist, whereof ye have heard that it should come; and even now already is in the world. (KJV)*

This attitude is one that denies Christ. Now many people say, "Well, if I ask someone, did Christ come in the flesh?" and they say "Yes," then they are okay. That's just part of the question. The other part is, He's coming in the flesh now. In *John 14:23*, let's go there, because I want to make this point very clear. Because if you don't understand this, you can ask that question, and still be deceived. It says in verse 23:

> *"Jesus answered and said to him, "If anyone loves Me, he will keep My word; and My Father will love him, and We will come to him and make Our home with him."*

Some translations say "abode," but it simply means, that the Father and Christ will be in you, and we know that in John 16 He is going to also send the Holy Spirit. So they are all going to be abiding in you. So when we read that statement in I John 4:3, it is saying, really, that you need to verify whether or not a person can confess that Christ literally came in the flesh and lived and was flesh and spirit, human and God, and that He also is constantly reproducing His mentality in us. Because we're supposed to have the mind of Christ, and the mind of Christ was the same as the mind of the Father. So if we have Him, we have the Father, the Son and the Holy Spirit abiding in us now. And an antichrist mentality will never confess that. They will never acknowledge that the Father, Son and the Holy Spirit is dwelling in you as a Christian. They cannot! The demon that is controlling that principality who manipulates the spirits that are under his control, in the antichrist arena, cannot do that.

So you need to understand that simply asking someone, "Do you believe Christ came?" and they say "yes", does not mean that they are not anti-Christ. Demons can acknowledge that, as the Scriptures say. They acknowledge, they believe, and they tremble, but they won't acknowledge that God is operating in you right now. They can't do it. They refuse to do it. So you need to understand. We need to spend more time in the Word of God, and not just superficially operating in the Word, knowing one or two scriptures, based on what somebody else told us about them, never have read them ourselves, not knowing what they mean, and not having the understanding that we need to have, in order to address some of the issues that need to be addressed in this spiritual battle.

Spirit of Error (64:48)

Now let's go to the spirit of error, which is usually a spirit that produces error, un-submissiveness, false doctrine, somebody who is unteachable, a servant of corruption, an individual who wants to be defensive and argumentative all the time, contentious, and the New Age Movement, this "New Age" thinking about "Well, God is everywhere, and in everything and we all have God, and God is in the toilet bowl and He's in all of these wonderful places." Let's turn to I John 4 and we go to verse 6 this time. It says, ***We are of God: he that knoweth God heareth us; he that is not of God heareth not us. Hereby know we the spirit of truth…"*** That's how we know the spirit of truth ***…and the spirit of error." (KJV)***

In other words, if you're hearing God, if I'm speaking the Word of God then you can hear me, then I can know where you're coming from. Now, how do you know if I'm speaking the Word of God? Well, I should be coming out of the Text of God, and you should be able to verify it. Now if you are not reading your Bibles, you won't know. Like I told my congregation, if I'm going to deceive you, you'll be deceived because you're not in the Word of God, and you're already deceived, and I'm just helping you in your deception because I'm already deceived. But if people are reading and studying and praying, and have a relationship with Jesus, Christ says, "My sheep hear my voice." So if you have a relationship with Christ, you're not going to be deceived perpetually and on-goingly, unless you are stooped in a spirit of error, there is sin in your life, and there's a corruption between you and Christ.

Spirit of Death (66:51 T-10)

Now let's move to the spirit of death. Death simply is an enemy, and death will be cast out. Revelation the 20th chapter. Death is an enemy of God's purpose, it's just that simple. God never intended death to enter in as a factor, sin brought death into the scenario.

Revelation 20:13 it says, *"The sea gave up the dead who were in it, and Death and Hades delivered up the dead who were in them. And they were judged, each one according to his works."*

So death is a reality, God is going to raise people up from their points of death. In verse 14 it says, *"Then Death and Hades were cast into the lake of fire. This is the second death."* So death was even cast into the lake of fire and destroyed. I Corinthians 15:26, again we'll see the attitude that God has toward death. And it says: *"The last enemy that will be destroyed is death."* And God will take care of death personally.

So my brothers and sisters we've dealt with a few of the enemies that attack us. We understand that we have power in Luke 10:17 to address these enemies, through prayer and fasting and having a relationship with God. With that in mind, move forward in power, love and a sound mind, and defeat the enemy that is trying to make himself prominent in your life.

Weapons of Our Warfare Section Three

I know that you have been equipped and inspired, and strengthened by these three CD's, (lecture), the collection called Weapons of Our Warfare. Continue to pray, study and fast, and solidify your relationship with God through the reading of His Word, and I will say, and you must remember, that you have the power, the love and sound mindedness given to you as stated in II Timothy 1:7. May God be with you, bless you, and give you the everlasting victory! AMEN.

Weapons of Our Warfare Section Three

References and Recommended Readings

Bloomer, George (1998). *Oppressionless*. Durham, NC.

Hammond, Frank and Ida Mae (1973). *Pigs in the parlor, a practical guide to deliverance*. Kirkwood, MO: Impact Christian Books, Inc..

Maddox, Dr. Ernest (2013). *Impact of a deliverance prayer, a study of deliverance ministry*. Oak Park, MI.

Maddox, Dr. Ernest (2013*). Apostolic manifesto, the God shift.* Oak Park, MI.

Robeson, Drs. Jerry and Carol (1985). *Strongman's his name… what's his game?*. New Kensington, PA.: Whitaker House.

Walker, Dr. Clarence (1996). *Breaking strongholds in the African American family, strategies for spiritual warfare.* Grand Rapids: Zondervan Publishing House.
.

Weapons of Our Warfare

Appendix A
Impact of a Deliverance Prayer

Chapter Two
Theory/Literature Review

The purpose of this Theory/Literature Review chapter will be to expose the reader to a sampling of the scope of literature/information relative to the issue of deliverance and spiritual warfare, with perspectives from a cross section of authors on the subject. Another purpose would be to lay the Biblical foundation and groundwork for the research that will respond to the question of this treatise/study.

Pre-History Cosmic Conflict

I must start this discourse with some quotes from Dr. Ed Murphy, from his book *The Handbook for Spiritual Warfare*, regarding cosmic rebellion.

> Freedom of choice was given Lucifer (if that was his name), and the angels, also. In the heavenly realm all of God's angels were evidently put to the test of obedience. Although the story of that test is nowhere recorded, it is everywhere implied. Those who withstood the deception of the fallen angel, possibly Lucifer (Isa. 14:12), were confirmed in holiness. They are described as the 'holy angels' (Mark 8:38) and the 'elect angels' (I Tim. 5:21, KJV). Those who were deceived and followed the rebellious Lucifer are now, like their master, confirmed in their iniquity. According to Scripture, no provision is made for their redemption. (Murphy, 1996, p. 25)

Dr. Murphy views this account as historic fact supported by Scriptures.

> This cosmic rebellion reached earth soon after man's creation. The evil it brought affected the universe on two levels: the natural and the moral. Edward J. Carnell defines *natural evil*

Appendix A
Impact of a Deliverance Prayer

> as 'all of those frustrations of *human values* which are perpetrated, not by the free agency of man, but by the *natural elements* of the universe, such as the fury of the hurricane and the devastation of the parasite.'... Carnell defines moral evil: '[It] includes all of those frustrations of human values which are perpetrated not by the natural elements in the universe, but by the free agency of man.' In his definitions of both natural and moral evil, Carnell limits his discussion exclusively to the relationship of evil to humanity. (Murphy, 1996, p. 5 - 26)

> With the introduction of humanity into the conflict between the two kingdoms, the formerly exclusive cosmic rebellion now becomes a cosmic-earthly rebellion. The historical- pictorial account is given in Genesis 3:1-24. The *historicity* of the Fall is confirmed in Scriptures such as 2 Corinthians 11:3 and Revelation 12:7-9. The historic fact of the Fall is also used by Paul in Romans 5 and I Corinthians 15 in connection with the historic, redemptive action of Jesus as the last Adam and the second man. I call Genesis 3 a pictorial account because of the vivid symbolism used to describe the historical events. The main truths of the story are just as real and historic if one admits to symbolism as they are if one follows a strict literalism. (Murphy, 1996, p. 27 - 28)

Bob Larson offers an interesting perspective regarding the cosmic conflict.

> Most Christians fail to view the battle for souls as a spiritual struggle based on exacting rules of procedure, established at the dawn of creation. The devil is like a lawyer in a cosmic courtroom, arguing his case where God is the judge, eternity is at stake, and the stiffest sentence is banishment forever from the presence of God. (Larson, 1999, p. 318)

Appendix A
Impact of a Deliverance Prayer

Larson presents this opinion without Biblical support, but the statement is consistent with the concept of Jesus Christ being our mediator and advocate. Refer to I Timothy 2:5, Hebrews 12:24, Hebrews 9:14,15.

In my opinion, Boyd in his statement captures the Western mindset relative to cosmic conflict, and how one can begin to address it.

> This is the truth to which the nearly universal intuition of spiritual warfare points. Thus from the perspective of Scripture, all the so-called primitive stories of cosmic conflict, and all the supposedly primitive techniques for waging war against evil spirits, must be judged as being far more true to reality than the Western "enlightened" Worldview, which presumptuously holds that the cosmos is strictly material, that no corporeal beings do not exist, and that humans are the highest form of life in the cosmos. If we can free ourselves from our own chrono-centrism, which is in reality another form of ethnocentrism, the heavily tinted nature of our Western Enlightenment spectacles will become apparent. (Boyd, 1997, p. 19 – 20)

I think Boyd identifies the problem relative to the primary obstruction to deliverance ministry/spiritual warfare, and the understanding of the cosmic conflict in Western culture.

The warfare begins as a cosmic conflict between Lucifer and God according to Dr. Murphy and became an earthly conflict. I agree with Dr. Murphy's overview of cosmic and post cosmic-earthly spiritual warfare perspective. I submit Isaiah 14: 12 – 15, and Ezekiel 28: 11 – 19, for review. It would be difficult to conclude that these verses refer to a human being, instead of Satan. I think it is important to present this concept as food for thought. The option to accept, reject, or ignore can be exercised.

Appendix A
Impact of a Deliverance Prayer

Spiritual Warfare
Deliverance Ministry History

Old Testament

Although this is not church history, per se, it is the earliest Biblical account of spiritual warfare according to Dr. Murphy. From my perspective, this establishes the first human encounter with what Dr. Murphy calls 'evil supernaturalism.'

> The major focus on spiritual warfare as experienced by humanity begins with Genesis 3. I will make no attempt to deal in any depth with the critical issues often raised about this story. As mentioned previously, Genesis 3 is both an historical and a pictorial account of the fall of humanity. It actually happened the way it is recorded. There really was an historical Adam and Eve. Not only were they the first human beings created in the image of God, but they stand as the representatives of the entire human race. Their transgression, particularly that of Adam as the head of the human race, is seen in Scripture as the fall of the human race (Rom.5; I Cor. 15). (Murphy, 1996, p. 34)

> Now the main teachings of the story about warfare with evil supernaturalism begins to unfold. We start with the danger of a two-way conversation, either verbally or within the mind, with the Devil on his terms. Satan began with the question, 'Has God indeed said...?' Instead of silencing him, Eve answered his question. He then subtly responded to her answer and their trap was set (Gen. 3:1 - 6). It is always dangerous to engage in a two-way dialogue with the Devil *on his terms.* To all of his doubts, lies, and boasts our response must be that of Jesus, 'Away with you, Satan! For it is written' (Matt. 4:10).'It is written' is equivalent to 'the sword of the Spirit, which is the word (rhema) of God' of Ephesians 6:17.

Appendix A
Impact of a Deliverance Prayer

> That is exactly how I handle demons in deliverance ministries. (Murphy, 1996, p. 35)

Spiritual warfare was not restricted to New Testament Church history; the backdrop from which this treatise has focused is New Testament spiritual warfare or deliverance. Satan was active in the Old Testament relative to opposing the human creation of God.

> And Satan stood up against Israel, and provoked David to number Israel. And David said to Joab and to the rulers of the people, Go, number Israel from Beersheba even to Dan; and bring the number of them to me, that I may know it. And Joab answered, The LORD make his people an hundred times so many more as they be: but, my lord the king, are they not all my lord's servants? why then doth my lord require this thing? why will he be a cause of trespass to Israel? (1Chronicles 21:1-3, KJV)

I do not want to spend more time extrapolating examples from the Old Testament when my focus is New Testament spiritual warfare Deliverance Prayer. But to ignore the area totally would not have been appropriate, from a Biblical perspective. I think it sets the backdrop for an Early Church deliverance history dialogue.

New Testament

The Early Church had a solid history of deliverance relative to demonic deliverance.

> The deliverance ministry was very manifest in the early church after Pentecost. Philip, the evangelist, was credited with working miracles. 'For unclean spirits crying with a loud voice, came out of many that were possessed with them' (Acts 8:6-7). Again Paul was grieved with the spirit of divination in the young girl who kept crying out, 'These men

Appendix A
Impact of a Deliverance Prayer

are the servants of the Most High God which show unto us the way of salvation' (Acts 16:16-18).

Today, many would applaud such utterances as great demonstrations of discernment. But Paul knew better, and after many days he commanded the spirit of divination to come out of her, and her vile employers lost their living. The evil spirit took the best part of an hour to obey the command of Paul. But finally, they had to yield to his authority. (Whyte, 1973, p. 80)

Spiritual Warfare
Deliverance Ministry History Overview

Francis MacNutt, in my opinion, provides one of the most compelling comprehensive brief Church deliverance ministry histories in the field. I will use quotes from his book *Deliverance from Evil Spirits* extensively to complete the historical deliverance, spiritual warfare overview. My approach is to comment sparingly between quotes for transitional connectivity, and to enhance the information delivery process.

Early Church History

Early Church history reveals that many, who may have not been ordained or part of the presbytery, but were part of the general body of believers, engaged in deliverance ministry.

In the early days of Christianity, all believers were assumed capable of praying for deliverance. Witness to this belief is the end of Mark's gospel, where the first of the five signs to 'accompany those who believe' is that 'in my name they will drive out demons' (Mark 16:17). Notice that those who perform deliverance here are not necessarily apostles or elders but ordinary believers. (MacNutt, 1995, p. 130)

Appendix A
Impact of a Deliverance Prayer

Early Church fathers documented the activities of spiritual deliverance (casting out demons) through prayer, or a simple adjuration that could be invoked by any Christian. The writers included names such as Origen, Justin Martyr, Irenaeus and Tertullian:

> The ministry of exorcism continued in the early Church. After Jesus' death Philip, the deacon ordained to oversee the distribution of bread, evangelized Samaria and made a great impact: 'With shrieks, evil spirits came out many' (Acts 8:7)
>
> After the death of the apostles, exorcisms were carried out with no mention of any special class of Christians to whom the ministry of deliverance was restricted. In fact, the Church father Origen (Martyred around A.D. 253) mentioned that many Christians cast out demons 'merely by prayer and simple adjurations which the plainest person can use. Because, for the most part, it is unlettered [or *illiterate*] persons who perform this work.' Origen added that exorcism does 'not require the power and wisdom of those who are mighty in argument.'
>
> Justin Martyr (who wrote earlier, around A.D. 150) states that 'many Christian men' exorcise demons that cannot be cast out by pagans. Women cast out demons, too, women like St. Eugenia in the third century.
>
> Incidentally, both Justin Martyr and Irenaeus (who wrote around A.D. 180) believed that Jews could perform exorcism in the name of the God of Abraham, Isaac and Jacob. Tertullian went so far as to say that the noblest Christian life is 'to exorcise evil spirits – to perform cures…to live to God. In his book *The Shows* he tried to convince pagans that there was more true enjoyment in casting out evil spirits and healing the sick than in attending the pagan plays and shows of the day. (Imagine a bishop encouraging his flock today to cast out evil spirits because it is more fun than seeing an R- rated movie!)

Appendix A
Impact of a Deliverance Prayer

> In all those early days we find no evidence that a Christian had to be ordained to cast out evil spirits. It was possible for any Christian to perform an exorcism. (MacNutt, 1995, p. 131)

Paul cast out demons Acts 16:6 –18 and Acts 19:11-12. Paul did not discuss what some might call exorcism among the gifts of the Holy Spirit. However, he did engage in spiritual deliverance warfare. Some accepted the premise that the gift of miracles included casting out demons.

> Nevertheless, Paul did not mention exorcism among the various manifestations (gifts) of the Holy Spirit enumerated in I Corinthians 12 – manifestations like 'gift of healing' (verse 9). Some believe that the gift of miracles (verse 10) might refer to exorcism. It makes sense that, just as some people are specially gifted by God with gifts of healing, other people might have gifts of exorcism. (MacNutt, 1995, p.132)

The power to cast out demons was not gender restricted in the Early Church.

> The Jesuit theologian Francisco Suarez (1548- 1617) pointed out that in the early Church, the power to cast out demons was given to all the faithful, both men and women. He also believed that the ability to exorcise the demon from a truly possessed person belonged to the order of miracles and should not be attempted 'without the special inspiration of the Holy Spirit. (MacNutt, 1995, p.132)

Note that Francisco Suarez referenced by MacNutt reinforced the concept that exorcism belonged to the order of miracles.

Narrowing of the Scope
The Church began to become narrow in the scope and practice of deliverance ministry and exorcism, limiting activity to specific groups of

Appendix A
Impact of a Deliverance Prayer

individuals. MacNutt suggests some reasons for the erosion of the scope relative to who should serve in the deliverance ministry activities.

> Over the course of centuries, several factors led to the gradual narrowing of exorcism to specially appointed group of exorcists. We can easily see why. For one thing, it is a difficult ministry. Even the apostles were unable to exorcise the epileptic demoniac, and they were rebuked by Jesus for being insufficiently prepared through prayer and fasting (Matthew 17:21).
>
> In more severe cases, insufficient spiritual protection can be dangerous to the exorcist. And if the exorcist does not know she is doing, it can be dangerous to the person being ministered to. Victims escaping from satanic covens are aware of this and afraid of approaching just any priest or minister for help. Their latter state could be worse than their first. (MacNutt, 1995, p. 133)

Perpetrators created a need to regulate deliverance ministry.

> As a result of these dangers, Cyprian wrote in the third century about a false prophetess who acted as if she were inspired by the Holy Spirit. Then an exorcist showed up, 'a man approved,' who discerned that she was really inspired by a wicked spirit, and not the Holy Spirit. Writes Evelyn Frost:
>
> This shows us that in the time of Cyprian there was an order of exorcists apparently regularized and approved by the Church. It is noteworthy that none of the 'very many brethren,' in spite of their strong faith, attempted to exorcise this woman, no one of the priests, but they appealed to the exorcist. This may be an indication that by the middle of the third century, the practice of exorcism in the Church had been open to abuse and required regularizing. (MacNutt, 1995, p.133)

Appendix A
Impact of a Deliverance Prayer

Problems also developed because in the Early Church history, baptism and exorcisms were connected relative to preparation for baptism (spiritual deliverance exorcism).

> Another fascinating factor related to the narrowing of exorcism to a specially appointed group of exorcists is that in the early days, adult baptism (usually at Easter or Pentecost) was preceded by a long preparation period, and exorcisms were always performed as part of that preparation. (It was assumed that most, if not all, pagans required freeing from demonic influence.) Sometimes these exorcisms were performed every day during the preparation period. (MacNutt, 1995, p. 133)

More and more restrictions appeared until by the tenth century formalization began to set in.

> Notice, too, that services by the tenth century were becoming increasingly formalized – 'by the book,' as it were. Already the exorcists may have been losing out on the creative possibility of working individually with each demonized person and making up prayers tailored to that person's needs, instead of repeating what was in the book. (MacNutt, 1995, p. 134)

Restrictions continued until the Middle Ages when priests became the ministers of deliverance and exorcisms. The process was eventually limited to priests in the twentieth century.

> Nevertheless, the exercise of deliverance ministry became more and more restricted (as things usually go in the history of the Church), until in the Middle Ages the priest became the normal minister of exorcism. Finally in our own century, in the time of Pope Pius XI, the ministry of exorcism was limited to the priest. (MacNutt, 1995, p. 135)

Appendix A
Impact of a Deliverance Prayer

Exorcism was deemphasized by Protestant Reformers. Laws were passed in some cases prohibiting exorcism.

> The Protestant Reformers, for the most part, deemphasized exorcism or did away with it altogether. Most Calvinists believed that exorcism was valid only in the early days of Christianity. Exorcism was connected in the Reformers' mind with Popish superstition, and although the Anglicans maintained a slim belief in a need for exorcism, their 1604 convocation passed a law 'which forbids any Anglican clergyman, without the express consent of his bishop obtained beforehand, to use exorcism in any fashion under any pretext, on pain of being counted an impostor and deposed from the ministry. (MacNutt, 1995, p. 135)

Some small pockets of deliverance ministry was practiced but basically deliverance ministry was not encouraged. For the most part, deliverance ministry was nonexistent or remote at best. "Still, the deliverance ministry has, over the centuries, been gradually shut down. In Protestant churches it has been almost abolished since, for the most part, few believe in the necessity" (MacNutt, 1995, p.137).

One of the main reasons for the caution and restrictions on deliverance ministry - exorcism was the abuse sometimes associated with the process (i.e. the Inquisition), and the belief of some that demonic possession may just be a psychotic manifestation.

> In 1709, for instance, in a reaction against the excesses and abuses of the Inquisition, the Vatican banned five manuals of exorcism, and in 1725 it instituted extensive controls.
>
> In 1972 Pope Paul VI dropped the four minor orders, including exorcist, as steps on the way to priestly ordination, with the assumption that *exorcist* was now obsolete as an order.
>
> Part of the reason for this drop-off of belief in the need for

Appendix A
Impact of a Deliverance Prayer

> exorcism was that experts in the field, like Fr. De Tonquedec, the official exorcist in Paris for half a century, claimed he was never convinced he had run up against a real case of possession. Instead, he said he thought that psychotics produced the symptoms of possession through their subconscious and through all the ceremonies surrounding exorcism. 'Call the devil and you'll see him; or rather not him, but a portrait made up of the sick man's ideas of him' was De Tonquedec's evaluation of his own work as official exorcist. Still in 1972 Pope Paul VI stoutly up held the traditional belief in Satan's existence. (MacNutt, 1995, p. 137)

Deliverance Resurgence
Contemporary State

The Pentecostals have been credited with the resurgence of deliverance ministry – exorcism in the twentieth century.

> Counter to the dying out of exorcism in the mainline churches, Catholic and Protestant, came the reawakening by Pentecostals of the supernatural gifts at the beginning of the twentieth century, including the power to cast out evil spirits.
>
> The baptism of the Spirit, praying in tongues, prophecy, healing and deliverance were all awakened in a powerful way not without problems, but certainly awakened.
>
> Emphasizing the priesthood of all believers, they did not separate the duties of clergy and laity in praying for deliverance. (MacNutt, 1995, p. 138)

The resurgence was not without problems and conflicts. Controls relative to who should perform or conduct deliverance ministry – exorcism and/or spiritual warfare reappeared. Open conflict developed between prominent individuals in the Christian arena, and Charismatic notables disputed about deliverance methodology.

Appendix A
Impact of a Deliverance Prayer

But as time went on, Pentecostal churches began to exercise more authority, with only evangelists, pastors and missionaries actually performing most of the exorcisms. The rediscovery of the need for many people to be free from demonic influence culminated in mass exorcisms – whole congregations of people under the ministry of non-denominational leaders like Derek Prince and Don Basham who taught extensively on the subject of spiritual warfare. Their mass exorcism ministry in the 1960s and '70s attracted large measure of criticism in charismatic circles, and David DuPlessis refused at times to appear on the same platform with them as a protest to their group exorcisms. Their position, though, was that exorcism had been neglected so long, and so many people needed it they had to do something, regardless of criticism, to help the many victims of demonic oppression. We were, as they saw it, in a crisis situation. (MacNutt, 1995, p.138)

Mainline churches have been impacted by the resurgence of deliverance ministry the same way they were impacted by the baptism of the Spirit doctrine just as the baptism of the Spirit and a lively understanding of the ministry of laypersons spilled out into the mainline churches through the influence of pioneers like the Episcopalian Rev. Dennis Bennett, so the gifts of healing and deliverance were introduced to mainline churches through leaders like Mrs. Agnes Sanford and the Rev. Alfred Price (one of the founders of the Order of St. Luke). (MacNutt, 1995, p.138)

Caution induced by fear has not permitted deliverance ministry to be received in the same way by mainline churches as praying in tongues, healing, and baptism in the Spirit has been received; deliverance ministry has been received with great reservation. Memories of the historical events in Salem and Medieval Europe were linked with historical and contemporary stories of failed exorcism, still breeds skepticism, control, fear, caution and disbelief.

Appendix A
Impact of a Deliverance Prayer

> Nevertheless, the deliverance ministry has been received by mainline denominations with more caution and criticism than the baptism in the spirit, healing and even praying in tongues. Deliverance is feared because of the disgraceful memories of the witch hunts of medieval Europe and the Salem witchcraft trials, coupled with recent horror stories of failed exorcism. In Germany twenty years ago, for example, two priests failed in their exorcism of a young woman, who ended up starving herself to death. The two priests and their imprudent exorcism were blamed for her death. In any case, caution rules in all the traditional churches. In some we even see a basic disbelief in the existence of the demonic realm. (MacNutt, 1995, p 139)

It was necessary to review the deliverance ministry from what was considered Pre Church – Pre New Testament period through the Deliverance Resurgence – Contemporary state. This review provided a backdrop historically for the dynamics associated with deliverance, exorcism, spiritual warfare and supernaturalism. More time could have been dedicated for the purpose of detail, but history is not the focus of this study. Deliverance Prayer relative to impact of a specific Deliverance Prayer is the focus. My belief is that a historical overview supports that focus.

Weapons of Our Warfare

Short Biography

Dr. Maddox has served God for over forty four years, and has been a leader in Youth Ministry, Radio Ministry, Satellite/TV, TCT (Total Christian Television) Leadership Training Ministry, and Inner Healing - Prayer and Deliverance Ministry. Dr. Maddox has served as a Deacon, Minister, and Elder. Dr. Maddox is currently the Pastor of the P.O.I.N.T.E. of Light Christian Center, which Jesus Christ led him to establish. Dr. Maddox is known nationally as a trainer, motivational speaker, and man of God in religious and secular arenas. Dr. Maddox is also President of Dr. E. Maddox Ministries. Dr. Maddox was called to be an Apostle by Jesus Christ, and this was confirmed by three men who are also Apostles.

Dr. Maddox has seen the power of God to save and deliver. God called him from a life of gang banging and drug dealing, to a life focused on helping others. God took a young man, with little more than a sixth grade education, and led him through a process from GED to Ph.D., and beyond. Dr. Maddox has earned these degrees, Bachelor of Science, Master of Arts/Business, Master of Public Administration, Doctor of Philosophy, Doctor of Ministry and Doctor of Education. Dr. Maddox has served as Dean of the Graduate Schools of Mission Leadership and Pastoral Leadership, at Destiny University in Ghana, Africa, and also served as an instructor at Power of the Word Bible College, Detroit MI. Dr. Maddox has served and taught the Word of God internationally in South Africa and Nigeria.

Dr. Maddox began his walk relative to Inner Healing and Deliverance Minis try over forty years ago. He was involved in a very conservative church organization from 1969 until 2000. What Jesus Christ was revealing to him was viewed as taboo in that environment. As a result Dr. Maddox had to rely on God the Father, Jesus Christ, the Holy Spirit and his wife, of over thirty seven years, Barbara.

"Weapons of Our Warfare", is a word for you and your deliverance. Dr. Maddox is available for consulting, training, teaching and preaching in all areas of ministry. Thank you for purchasing this book.

"His Kingdom Come; Amen"

Weapons of Our Warfare

www.ingramcontent.com/pod-product-compliance
Lightning Source LLC
Chambersburg PA
CBHW071301040426
42444CB00009B/1825